2/8 .22.78

Bob Gibson on Lou Brock: "He's the best damn money player I ever saw. . . . He's a superpsych."

Stan Musial on Lou Brock: ". . . the most exciting baseball player in the major leagues over the last ten years."

Ernie Banks on Lou Brock: "Then all of a sudden he leaps, and *you* sit there, wonderin' how anyone can move from zero velocity to the speed of light like that. . . . It was like there must have been some frames missin' from the TV film."

Against the backdrop of these accolades, it is surprising to learn that Louis C. Brock of the St. Louis Cardinals got into baseball almost by accident. In fact, Brock came to baseball from a background very different from the standard Little League, hot dog, competition-minded middle-class America that we know today. STEALING IS MY GAME is the story of Brock's life from his childhood as a sharecropper's son to his manhood as the holder of the record for bases stolen for one season.

Brock, a certain Hall of Famer, who fought contradictions and stereotypes from the very beginning, talks about what it was like to be a young ballplayer — a thinking ballplayer with enormous potential who was so uptight he kept "tripping over his own brains." He tells what it felt like to be traded, a career lowpoint that turned out to be a blessing in disguise;

(continued on back flap)

faced and the ones who have earned his respect.

The very personal story of a truly great athlete, STEALING IS MY GAME takes the reader into the rough-and-tumble world of professional baseball — the game, the players, the managers, the reporters, and the fans who have all had their effect on the making of Lou Brock, ballplayer extraordinary.

STEALING IS MY GAME by Lou Brock & Franz Schulze

PRENTICE-HALL, INC., ENGLEWOOD CLIFFS, N.J.

DEDICATION

Lou Brock
For Wanda Lorraine and Louis C., Jr.

Franz Schulze
For Matthew and Luke

Art Director: Hal Siegel

Stealing Is My Game
by Lou Brock and Franz Schulze
Copyright © 1976 by Louis Brock
All rights reserved. No part of this book may be reproduced in any form or
by any means, except for the inclusion of brief quotations in a review,
without permission in writing from the publisher.
Printed in the United States of America
Prentice-Hall International, Inc., London
Prentice-Hall of Australia, Pty. Ltd., Sydney
Prentice-Hall of Canada, Ltd., Toronto
Prentice-Hall of India Private Ltd., New Delhi
Prentice-Hall of Japan, Inc., Tokyo
Prentice-Hall of Southeast Asia Pte. Ltd., Singapore
10 9 8 7 6 5 4 3 2 1

LIBRARY OF CONGRESS CATALOGING IN PUBLICATION DATA

Brock, Lou,
    Stealing is my game.

    1. Brock, Lou,   2. Baseball.   I. Schulze,
Franz,   joint author.   II. Title.
GV865.B72A33   796.357'092'4   [B]   76–17051
ISBN 0–13–846378–6

The subject being Brock, I decided to look up the word. One dictionary defines "brock" as a kind of badger; another as a nasty or contemptible fellow. That doesn't help at all.

Many times, surely, the men Lou Brock has played baseball against must have been willing to associate him with the first of those meanings, but with the second, never. Troublesome, persistent, harassing, yes, infinitely so; a rascal—a *brock,* that is—no way.

You begin to see the problem. Lou Brock is not easy to catch or even to fix in your sights. You know he is one of the very best ballplayers of the past quarter century, and I can't think of more than two or three who were as beautiful to watch, as interesting or as accomplished. You can sit through a major-league game which by normal standards is atrociously played overall and going exactly the wrong way for you. But if Brock is in it the odds are 10–1 it will be worth paying good money to see.

Statistics bear this out, but only somewhat. The qualities about him that remain with you have to do less with figures than with style, and the style itself defies generalization. This is at the heart of it: That you never feel quite safe with any summing-up of the talents you presume he possesses in abundance.

Or does he? He is a very good hitter, with the keenest of eyes and a panther's grace at the plate. The writers assure you of that. But he strikes out a lot. He once had ambitions to be a slugger, yet he never realized them in the big leagues. So, just when you decide the long ball is not his virtue, that he hasn't got the wrists for it, or the weight or something, he hits a shot into the center-field stands at the Polo Grounds that travels farther than all but a few legendary home runs in the history of the game.

Brock himself has said, "I am not Willie Mays with the glove," but the chief reason I so vividly recall a catch he made of a liner by Bill Madlock at Wrigley Field last year (1975) is that I know—because I saw it on film three times after it happened —that it was not possible for anyone to catch that ball. I still believe it was not. Don Kessinger had hit one like it the previous season in the same place—beyond Brock's reach, but Brock reached it.

Everybody says he is murder on the basepaths, right? But he is not so fast as half a dozen other men playing today (he loves to admit it), and what he does so dramatically, he studiously endeavors to do with a minimum of drama.

One thing is beyond doubt. He will worry you to death if you play against him, yet by means that change from day to day. He'll drive to the power alleys, then poke spinners to the opposite field, bunt you dizzy and steal you blind. Or he'll kill your own rally with some impossibly lovely caper in the field.

Another thing: He knows all this about himself, and it has been nurtured with the analytical self-consciousness of an intellectual, but he never appears to be, in fact I know he never is, thinking a great deal about himself.

Yet another thing: It is a pleasure akin to that of watching ballet to see him on the field, walking with that lightly oiled, faintly duck-footed but smashingly attractive looseness of his, say, from the dugout to the on-deck circle.

And finally: He is good with people, but he can't dance worth a nickel. And on the one occasion someone tried to teach him to swim as an adult, he dropped like a stone, straight to the bottom of the Atlantic Ocean.

Franz Schulze

Introduction

"Yeah, I agree with all you say, or most of it, but I want to qualify it. Lou sociable? Sure. Do his teammates look up to him? Of course they do. But it's not because he's what you'd call a leader. Anybody who's been around as long as he has with one club and who plays as well as he plays is bound to have people respecting him, but not because he looks good on a soapbox carrying a flag in his hand. He does it all quietly, on a person-to-person basis. He's lots of laughs and he looks gregarious, but you must have heard him say—because he's been quoted a lot saying it—'When I'm angriest, I smile the most.' It's true.

"I'll tell you what to put in your book. Tell 'em what Brock is best at. It's not hitting or stealing bases. It's not records, although

I know how much he thinks about records. That's one of the reasons he knows the averages so well. He's the best damn money-player I ever saw on the Cardinals. Maybe he's the best ever, though I can't tell about players on other teams. You have to live with a man day in and day out to know how good he is in the clutch. Anybody can have a big day or a great World Series once in a while, but Lou never misses when there's money riding. He's a superpsyche. He rises to occasions like nobody I ever saw on that team.

"I was never like that. I had a couple of good Series, but they followed pretty good years, and even the time I struck out those seventeen Tigers, I think that was mostly because I was unfamiliar to Detroit. With Lou, the other team knows perfectly well what he's going to do, but he goes ahead and does it anyhow. In fact, he does it best when they know he's going to do it.

"It's no accident, either. He's done it too many times to chalk it up to chance. When you come down to the end of a season and you need a hit or a run, Brock is who you look to, and he usually gets it for you. It's uncanny. I don't know why he's that way. Of course he's competitive, but that only describes the same thing in another way. I guess it's inborn. That's what you say about a guy when you can't explain why he is the way he is.

"Same thing applies to the way he plays with pain. One year he finished up the season with a goddam broken shoulder. They X-rayed it and found his shoulder was broken. He was playing well too.

"That's one of the reasons he has nearly 3,000 hits, and why he gets about 200 hits every year and always steals fifty bases or more.

"On the other hand, I suspect all the talk about his consistency and his thinking-every-minute nature gets carried too far at times. Some of the things that have been written about him are clichés. I've seen him take long leads off first, in spite of what all you writers say about the famous short Brock lead. He does it against lefthanders. Watch him closely with them some time. And I've seen him pull a rock more than once. He's not all *that* calculating. He'll now and then do something crazy or on impulse, just like the rest of us. He's no machine. He just won't admit to making mistakes, which doesn't mean he doesn't make them. I personally think he should have slid on that throw to the plate by Willie Horton in the '68 World Series. I told him so. He didn't admit it to me then and he won't to anybody now. You can't hold it against him; it's a sign of quality. Just remember: For every time he's done something that violates common sense, he's done 200 things that are exactly on target. That's how the clichés about his calculating temperament get started.

"But look at the way he strikes out. That's hardly the sign of a thoughtful, deliberating kind of guy. Almost all hitters who have either high home-run totals or plus-.300 batting averages strike out more than they need to. That's 'cause they swing at balls as well as strikes, at anything that comes within their zone. They're eager to hit. A real sharp-eyed hitter, the kind who can distinguish a ball from a strike, may give a pitcher a lot of trouble, but he seldom hits more than .270. The higher averages belong to the guys who are aggressive.

"At the same time I don't want to create the impression he's an emotional ballplayer either. Of course he thinks things out. Sometimes, in fact, he strikes out because he thinks too much, 'cause he's trying to outsmart the pitcher. He's at his best when his adrenaline is flowing at about the same rate as his thinking.

"He's learned how to hit too. Once he was a slugger, remember? Then he became more of a line-drive hitter and he started stealing bases. So people forgot about the home runs. Later on he learned how to bunt, how to pop one to the opposite field. So he's been able to keep his average right around .300 over the years, even though he can't hit for power the way he used to.

"He's thirty-seven. The hitting begins to go along about that time if you don't figure out ways of making up for it. Everything goes. Everything begins to tail off. I should know. And that's why I admire his determination—and his ability—to hang in there and adjust, more than I'm impressed by all the records. He wouldn't have the records except for the ability to adjust and keep himself alive.

"He'll break Cobb's record. Sure he's slower now than he used to be. But remember, Brock fully two steps slowed down is still as fast as everybody else, and everybody else doesn't have his will. If he doesn't break the record in 1976, he'll do it in 1977. He'll just play until he does it. All he needs is forty bases a year for two years, and he can steal forty bases running backward.

"Is he Hall of Fame material? Be serious. How can you ask? How can he miss? Besides, like I said, I never gave that much of a damn about records myself, and I'm not all that impressed by the Hall of Fame. If anything, there are too many guys in it already, guys who got voted in when the standards were lax or just because the writers were dewy-eyed about them.

"And that reminds me of Brock in the 1974 Most Valuable Player voting. He should have won it. And from his standpoint he had a right to be pissed off that he didn't. Yes, Garvey was on a pennant-winning team, and yes, he had the L.A. press going for him. If Lou had been playing in New York, even a Dodger pennant wouldn't have kept him from getting the award. Hype is damned important.

"But that's not the real factor in my mind. It was race.

"Lou was black and Garvey was white. When you get two good men going against each other who are about equal in ability, it's the white guy that'll get the honor, 99% of the time.

"Black players have still got a tough time of it. I'm not saying it isn't better now than it used to be. It *is* better, especially among the players themselves. In fact you can't find a more beautiful resolution of the race problem than among the players themselves. The tensions are almost totally gone there now. But they're still evident, in subtler form maybe, but still evident, among management, the press and the fans. That's what hurt Lou in '74. Of course he won't admit that either. He doesn't talk much about the race thing, though I know he has strong feelings about it. I have strong feelings too, only I'm hard-assed. I'll talk about it and I won't take shit.

"But anyhow, you asked about Lou and the MVP, not about race. Here's why he should have won that award. To begin with, what's it fundamentally for? It's supposed to be given to the guy who is the most productive, most exciting player in the league . . . the most valuable.

"Well, if you were to put two teams in a couple of games at the same time on opposite sides of the same town—in 1974—and if Lou Brock were in one of those games, I *know* that one would outdraw the other by 20,000 fans. People knew what they were likely to see—Brock stealing a base—and that was the most exciting thing in baseball that year. With all due respect to Garvey, what turned on the fans was the prospect of seeing Lou out there, getting on base, then worrying the pitcher with that dance of his, then taking off and beating the catcher's throw to second. They wanted to see him more than they wanted to see Garvey get a hit or drive in a run.

"Lou was all electricity in 1974. He hit and he ran, beautifully and productively, and he was a turn-on at the same time.

"I will admit he is not the best outfielder God ever made. He hasn't got the hands. He can follow a fly ball and get to it as well as anybody and better than most, but he doesn't always know what to do with it when he reaches it. I mean he drops it sometimes. You aren't supposed to drop it; you look better if you hang onto it. He always had that problem, although he used to make up for it somewhat with a terrific arm that he'd still have today if he hadn't racked himself up with injuries so much.

"Even so, he's always been amazing to watch, even when he does things Joe DiMaggio or Curt Flood wouldn't have done.

"First year he was with the Cardinals, we were in Milwaukee one night. I was pitching, I recall, and one of the Braves hit a tall fly right down the left-field line. Lou took off. To his left. Exactly in the wrong direction. Then he suddenly realized what he was doing and reversed himself and ran like an antelope toward that fly ball, which was sinking fast. He leaped up and caught the damn thing, and as we were coming back into the dugout, Bill White said to me, 'So that's Brock, huh? Well, he's either the best or the worst outfielder I ever saw.' That sums him up in the field. Even then, he's at least damned interesting.

"And like I say, he's more than that when the Cardinals are

up. He just wants to be the best ballplayer alive. Not a bad ambition for a thirty-seven-year-old man.

"What? You say he looks damned good for a thirty-seven-year-old man? Hell, you should have seen me."

Bob Gibson

Contents

LOUIS CLARK BROCK

Year	Club	AVG.	G	AB	R	H	2B	3B	HR	RBI	BB	SO	SB
1961	St. Cloud	.361	128	501	117	181	33	6	14	82	51	105	38
	Chicago	.091	4	11	1	1	0	0	0	0	1	3	0
1962	Chicago	.263	123	434	73	114	24	7	9	35	35	96	16
1963	Chicago	.258	148	547	79	141	19	11	9	37	31	122	24
1964	Chicago	.251	52	215	30	54	9	2	2	14	13	40	10
	St. Louis	.348	103	419	81	146	21	9	12	44	27	87	33
1965	St. Louis	.288	155	631	107	182	35	8	16	69	45	116	63
1966	St. Louis	.285	156	643	94	183	24	12	15	46	31	134	74
1967	St. Louis	.299	159	689	113	206	32	12	21	76	24	109	52
1968	St. Louis	.279	159	660	92	184	46	14	6	51	46	124	62
1969	St. Louis	.298	157	655	97	195	33	10	12	47	50	115	53
1970	St. Louis	.304	155	664	114	202	29	5	13	57	60	99	51
1971	St. Louis	.313	157	640	126	200	37	7	7	61	76	107	64
1972	St. Louis	.311	153	621	81	193	26	8	3	42	47	93	63
1973	St. Louis	.297	160	650	110	193	29	8	7	63	71	112	70
1974	St. Louis	.306	153	635	105	194	25	7	3	48	61	88	118
1975	St. Louis	.309	136	528	78	163	27	6	3	47	38	64	56
MAJOR TOTALS		.295	2130	8642	1381	2551	416	126	138	737	656	1509	809

WORLD SERIES RECORD

Year	Club	AVG.	G	AB	R	H	2B	3B	HR	RBI	BB	SO	SB
1964	St. Louis	.300	7	30	2	9	2	0	1	5	0	3	0
1967	St. Louis	.414	7	29	8	12	2	1	1	3	2	3	7
1968	St. Louis	.464	7	28	6	13	3	1	2	5	3	4	7
SERIES TOTALS		.391	21	87	16	34	7	2	4	13	5	10	14

ALL-STAR GAME RECORD

Year	Club	AVG.	AB	R	H	2B	3B	HR	RBI	BB	SO	SB
1967	National	.000	2	0	0	0	0	0	0	0	0	0
1971	National	.000	1	0	0	0	0	0	0	0	0	0
1972	National					DID NOT APPEAR						
1974	National	1.000	1	1	1	0	0	0	0	0	0	1
1975	National	.333	3	1	1	0	0	0	0	0	0	1
ALL-STAR TOTALS		.286	7	2	2	0	0	0	0	0	0	2

I. Springtime

The story begins on a ninety-foot stretch of Florida dirt, in an amiable old dump of a St. Petersburg ballpark called Al Lang Field. Lou Brock of the St. Louis Cardinals is standing with his left foot lightly perched on first base. There are two outs in the bottom of the third inning of an exhibition game between St. Louis and the Chicago White Sox. Brock has just stroked a looping single over the head of the Sox second baseman, Jorge Orta.

The crowd stirs. *Maybe Lou will do it for us now. . . .*

The Sox had been treating the Cardinals uncharitably that warm March afternoon in 1975. They had already scored five runs in their three turns at bat and their big pitcher, Wilbur Wood, despite heaps of winter fat added to a middle which is normally monumental anyhow, had been disposing of St. Louis batsmen with an executioner's cold skill. Brock was the first Redbird to hit safely off him. Since St. Pete is the Cardinals' spring-training camp, the townsfolk are loyal to them. Yet the buzz running through the grandstand now hardly seemed warranted, given a five-run home deficit, two down and one lonely runner on first base.

It was the runner at issue, however, not the game. By standards of attentiveness, Brock, who stole 118 bases in 1974 and set the baseball world on its ear doing it, was the unloneliest man in the park. All the eyes in Al Lang Field were on him, and the two belonging to Wilbur Wood were easily the most mindful, the most solicitous. Wilbur stretched and glared at Lou, imperiously, like a turn-of-the-century lawyer, with that great paunch. Brock had moved no more than three feet from the bag before Wood reared and fired to the first baseman.

The gesture was a tribute to Brock and it gained him a psychological advantage before he had made any move of his own. Wood wasn't sure his opponent meant to steal second, but he knew full well he could, and the knowledge victimized him. He threw three times to first base before offering anything to batter Ted Sizemore. Brock meanwhile never strayed farther than a couple of bats' lengths from the bag.

At last Wood delivered to Sizemore, who took the pitch for a ball. Brock had increased his lead to two-and-a-half steps. Wilbur urged him back to the bag with a hurried throw.

I was watching this, the first spring-training game I had ever seen, from the box seats behind home plate. Next to me sat Buck O'Neil, the venerable scout of the Chicago Cubs. "Sure he's gonna go," said Buck. "If Wilbur is that worried about him, Lou can't afford to disappoint him, much less the rest of us."

Wood stared with unconvincing impassivity toward first, where Brock was now beginning to move about a little, and gradually more and more. Lou hitched up his pants, feinted toward second just once, then even before Wood could respond to the challenge ambled back to first. He put his hands on his waist, then on his knees. He spread his feet and let his arms dangle down, with his hips shifting languidly from side to side. He kicked the bag and sidled away from it again. None of these moves, with the exception of the feint, was quick, impulsive or startling; just restless and unrepetitive.

Wood never relaxed his vigilance; he was like a man poised with a fly-swatter. Once more he addressed Sizemore. His left heel turned just a hair, digging almost imperceptibly into the dirt.

Movement now, a flashing of red and white on the baseline between first and second. I would like to say Brock took off like a shot, but that is not the right metaphor. One moment he was almost loafing, the next he was driving down to second, legs pounding like pistons, but if the transition was quick, it was nevertheless too smooth, if you can believe that, for the start of his run to be called explosive. Catcher Ed Herrmann reacted alertly and threw accurately to second. The fly-swatter came down, but the fly makes decisions and moves in just about the same fraction of a second it took Brock to beat the throw. Wood looked on helplessly.

So did I. I was down in St. Petersburg to take notes about Lou Brock the baseball player, the great baseball player, as it is fully established by now: accomplished hitter (even sometime eye-popping slugger), graceful outfielder, 100-proof marvel in the clutch, above all base-stealer *sans pareil* . . . successor to Wills, heir to Cobb, model to today's younger comets—Morgan, Lopes, Cedeno—and, well, maybe Lou Brock is just the best baserunner of all time.

The ideal way of getting into my project, I thought, would be right away to watch him in his famous act of larceny. I had seen him do it before, of course—countless times against the team I root for, the customarily hapless Chicago Cubs. But I had never really studied what he did. He had; moreover, he had talked about it with me for hours a few days before, on tape, with an analytical thoroughness and a precision of articulation that led me to wonder what kind of a solid college teacher he would have been had he set his mind to it. He was a math major at Southern University, I recalled, and his habit of thinking was to break any problem down into its components, quantify them if possible, order all variables and exhaust all data pertinent to it. He had talked about walking back from second to first base after unsuccessful attempts at stealing, and over and over again examining his cleat marks to see what he could learn from them about variations in the pressure of footprints, deviations from what ought to be an absolutely straight running line, optimal points for takeoff, acceleration and slides, and God knows what all. He had the whole act clocked, with so many tenths of a second presumed for the pitch to reach the plate, so many for the catcher to catch the pitch and throw back to second, or to first for a pitchout, or for him to take off from exactly how many steps of a lead, to use up how many strides down the line before sliding how many feet into the bag. He discussed the advantages and the difficulties of stealing with a pull hitter at the plate, or a singles hitter, or a left-handed batter or a rightie, or off Tom Seaver or Andy Messersmith, on a fastball or a curve, on inside or outside pitches, or with a popup slide or a hook, and on and on and on.

The complexity of his arithmetic was matched by the subtlety of his psychology. He could hang out a shingle and make good money telling his opponents how much he knew about their mental habits and how much he capitalized on the knowledge—except that he makes more by keeping the information from them.

He had given me a crash course in what he was up to, and the contents were tumbling about in my brain the moment he broke that day against Wilbur Wood. In truth, very little of his instruction helped me to understand how he did what he did. His lead was too short, even for him. He was fast down to second, all right, but not as fast as a couple of other players I saw during the same spring-training stint—his own teammate Bake McBride and the Detroit Tigers' Ron Le Flore. There was really nothing spectacular about what he had done—no fancy ballet at first base, no long tantalizing leads or dramatic bellyflops back to first, no grand, earthmoving slide into second. All he seemed to have done was exact a safe sign from the umpire at second base, and I can still remember Jorge Orta doing little circles near the bag, just after Brock's caper, looking as if he was trying to figure it out himself.

Well, I know more about it now, or at least enough to tell you later what Lou told me about the meticulous pains and microscopic detail that go into the art of stealing bases in major-league baseball.

But Lou is more than a sprinter or a basepath student of Einstein and Freud. He is a player with a record of all-round achievements that include seasons like 1964, when he made the Cubs and Yankees weep—the one for letting him get away, the other for letting him get too close—or like 1967 and 1968, when he carried off World Series performances against Boston and Detroit that will be the fuel of hot-stove-league discussions for longer than most of us will be around to enjoy.

There is a lot yet to tell, and for me, on that day in March of 1975, there was a lot yet to learn. The mysteries of the stolen base and the special fascination of the whole Brock could wait, while I had my first fascinated look at baseball from a vantage point closer than a box seat on the first-base line.

The clubhouse at Al Lang Field is something less than a jewel of the interior decorator's art. It is clean and decent, but minimally appointed; cramped, well-worn, an altogether unimpressive space after you've seen it once.

Ah, but the first time! Then it is an authentic object of awe, though mostly because you've never been in the likes of it before, and all the romance of Big Time that has accumulated in your head over the years now transfigures this modest knockabout room where the thirty men who perform in the field for the St. Louis National League entry prepare themselves daily for their professional activities. When you first step into it, you are nine years old again with no college degrees or mortgages, and the thirty men have resumed the status of semidivinity they had when you were just beginning to read about the major leagues in the newspapers. And Lou Brock, whom you came down here specially to visit, is for a moment a god among these demigods, fleet Mercury, and past mortality. For a little while, the Al Lang Field clubhouse is Olympus.

Not that either, really. Neither gods nor even gladiators, they are just a bunch of soiled men with their clothes off, and collectively not especially handsome. You mention this to Brock, the only one you know sufficiently to ask, and who is built well enough anyway to be exempt from the generalization—you say, how come there is so much lard leaking out over the belts, so many pear shapes, sloping shoulders and cases of residual acne, not only among coaches in their fifties, but among these big beautiful deals who are supposed to be such physical specimens?

And Lou reminds you that it is not really a fast game most of the time, like basketball, where you are constantly locomoting at high velocity. In baseball you sit and stand around a lot. Besides, it's March right now (although the fact is, we aren't going to look that much better in September). Anyway, you just got here, man. You haven't seen these guys in action yet. They move pretty good when they need to.

At the moment, nonetheless, they are moving slowly, and when they talk, it is in half-sentences and low tones. No banter or very little of it; banter is for the morning and the game, evidently not for now. For now they sit on their stools in front of their lockers, very thoughtfully and deliberately peeling off their complicated uniforms with all the layers and tabs and slots and overlaps. Next, the showers, and again, forget Olympus. The shower room is rude, stark, in need of paint and evidently of the benefit of more water pressure, judging from the sign over the latrines (by now brimming with urine of deepest gold), which prohibits flushing until the showers are empty.

So this is the big leagues and these the deities of my youth. Hardly godlike here, I guess, yet not all the worship is out of me. I recall fishing from a wastebasket a cheaply printed green card with the St. Louis B batting order written hastily on it in the hand of Red Schoendienst. Himself. I will salvage it for my two preadolescent sons, but if I find another like it tomorrow I will keep it for my own files.

In the same wastebasket is the refuse from the refreshment table, which features plastic casks of strawberry drink and lemonade; boxes of Big Red chewing tobacco and Bazooka Bubble Gum; a stack of Campbell's soup; an electric can-opener, wooden matches. (Why these and not something else?) And there are the equipment bags. Each player has one and it rests, or rather slouches, on top of his locker. It is usually a beatup thing and beautiful for being old, because it is issued early in his career to each major-leaguer, who keeps on using it even after he is traded to another club. So the names of the Giants, the Cubs, the Angels and how many others decorate the clubhouse of the St. Louis Cardinals. Everybody is a gypsy here and no one a virgin. You begin to know a little more about the professionalism of big-time sports, the rough road and the toughened feet that tread it, or fail to for want of toughness.

As a matter of fact, that recognition is reinforced by seeing these weary men put themselves together now, after a long day, in silence, usually, and in some cases, no doubt, thinking thoughts they cannot share. There across the room is Claude Osteen, the once superb lefthander for the Los Angeles Dodgers whose pitching magic has deserted him the last two seasons. If the writers are wondering whether it will come back to him this year in St. Louis, what do you suppose he is wondering? Or Eddie Brinkman, the sort of player who tends to be slapped, cruelly, I daresay, with the cliche "journeyman," but who, you know when you see him three days later against the Tigers, is capable of scintillating work afield. Well, he's thirty-three . . . a glove gets you just so far . . . how much further now? . . . how much longer?

Even the great Gibson: Now, there's a subject to conjure with. This book will be about Lou Brock, and Lou Brock, as I have every intention of spelling out, is one of the genuinely memorable ones, in personality as well as skill. But it is Gibson who exudes the hottest charisma on this ballclub. If he isn't the most intelligent man on the roster, I cannot name his superior.

Moreover, it is a big, spirited intelligence, ferocious, verbal, vain, ignited by a rebellious wit and undergirded with a ton of physical talent. Not the biggest, he is yet the most powerful figure in the clubhouse: six feet three, with a massive torso stacked on two long, skinny legs, a barrel on stilts. His face is mahogany and his eyes are black bullet holes under lowering brows. The face falls easily into what seems a scowl if not a sneer, and physically he must be the scariest-looking cat on the mound of all the pitchers of his day. I have only the faintest idea of what he is like back of this splendid, off-putting facade, for I haven't talked to him much and he is not only proud but obviously complex enough to discourage superficial analysis. But he is something to watch and listen to. And everybody listens, partly because he is such a tree of a man, partly because he is voluble and immensely interesting. He talks a lot, and what he says crackles. He likes to fling his bolts across the room at Lou, I think because he likes Lou, because he knows Lou is his equal in brains, and will give back as good as he gets.

But Gibson is no colt anymore. The years are adding up, and the fastball that a few seasons ago could take your nose right off your face is not so zippy now. He has his grandeur to fall back upon—something Eddie Brinkman hasn't—but Gibson is also possessed of the kind of animal competitiveness that can't feed on memories all that comfortably, at least not yet. His best defense against waning force is his intelligence, undoubtedly, but even that is not likely to prevent him from wondering now at 5:30 P.M. on March 12, whether he will live up to the standards this year (he's starting Saturday against Detroit) that his own grandeur has imposed upon him.

These are, or I reckon must be, the thoughts of the older guys in the clubhouse. And what of the young? What of Keith Hernandez, twenty-three, unscarred, classically handsome in the Mediterranean style, the hope of the Cardinals to fill the first-base shoes of the brilliant Joe Torre, now gone to the Mets. Surely a burden lies heavy on him, and it figures to get heavier about three o'clock of an occasional sleepless morning.

That's a strange name for a Hernandez, Keith. The two parts don't fit the way "Luis" fits "Melendez" or "Hector" works with

"Cruz," which reminds me of yet another unolympian aspect of life in the Cardinal clubhouse. It is the Latins, not the blacks, who are the isolates in this subculture called a professional ballclub. The Latins often huddle together in the clubhouse and the dugout, talking Spanish with each other and English with hardly anyone else, and you sometimes sense an acute melancholy among them, especially if they are kids. In the hip, breezy, nothing-if-not-secular atmosphere of the clubhouse (early in the day, anyhow, if not as late as now), it is touching to see a blood-young Puerto Rican boy sitting next to his locker, alone and in silence, reading from a dogeared paper back copy of *El Nuevo Testamento*.

On the diamond and from the average fan's vantage point, all these guys look like well-formed, swaggering adults. And why not? They get their names in the newspapers and their faces on the Johnny Carson show; they are national products. Sixty-year-old executives on vacation in Florida come up to them in the lobby of the Sheraton Bel-Air, deference in their manner, autograph books in their hands. Yet the young Cardinals are the age of undergraduates or just barely past it, and their glamorous but merciless livelihood doesn't reduce the vulnerability of their years all that much. I think of McBride again, whose credentials are already impressive by any established big-league standard; excellent glove man, whippet on the bases, an already feared hitter who, Lou Brock once said to me, might conceivably break .400 someday, if he stays free of injuries. A substantial young man, sure enough; yet one afternoon in St. Pete, after a ballgame, as Brock was submitting to a cortisone shot in the knuckles, McBride happened by and watched the scene in nauseated horror. "Oh, Christ!" he said, grimacing at the sight of the needle going deep into Brock's hand. "That's terrible. Terrible." Making light of it, the doctor removed the needle, looked up at Lou's black face and said, "Hey, you just paled perceptibly." Laughs all around. But not from McBride.

The morning is a lot different than the afternoon. The mood is high, especially among these 1975 Cardinals, who figure they have a lively shot at the pennant. They missed it by an eyelash last year, when my Cubs—hapless, you remember I called them—swooned to the Pirates on the last day of the season and Pittsburgh eased into the divisional title. But now the winter is over, the Florida sun is high in the sky, the team has arrived in Lakeland, shortly before noon, for a game with the Tigers, and the midday energy is finding its way out of the players' mouths.

Ron Fairly was dressing a few feet away from Lou Brock. Both men are veterans, with lots of memories worth trading, although Fairly hardly needs to wait for the other man's move. He goes on and on without priming. This time his reminiscences covered his days with the Dodgers: "So Drysdale gets himself in this jam, see? And Alston tells him to walk Clendenon. 'Hell,' Drysdale says to himself, 'I don't need no four pitches to get the sonofabitch on base. I can do it in one.' And he nails Clendenon in the ribs on the next throw, which was a hard fastball. Well, I can tell you Alston was mad and he let Drysdale know it, but Drysdale just smiled at him and says, 'Look at it this way. It was a good deal easier on my arm, and anyhow it put some respect in him the next time he come up.'

"Hey, Lou, remember Tony Taylor? Used to cross himself every time he came up to bat. Made the sign of the cross. Well, I recall one day he was hitting against Gibson, and Gibbie, as you know, doesn't have much truck with any of that Jesus jazz, so he shows his back to Taylor and crosses *him*self, then turns around and yells, 'O.K., Taylor, now we gonna see which side Big Daddy is on.' "

Overhearing Fairly, pitching coach Dave Ricketts now decided it was time to ride Gibson, who had just sauntered into the dressing room as Fairly was finishing his tale. "How in hell did Gibson ever *see* Taylor?" Ricketts asked, for Gibson's benefit, not Fairly's. "With his eyes, he can't even see a catcher's sign."

"You forget about my glasses," said Gibson indulgently. "When I got my glasses on, as far as I am from you, Ricketts, I can see a gnat pissin' in a piece of cotton."

Brock liked that one, and he chuckled audibly enough for Gibson to become aware of him. "Listen to Brock, will you?"

Gibson went on. "He laughs at anything. I mean anything. That's how sophisticated *he* is. You can take 'em out of the bushes, but that don't mean you can get the hay out of their hair.

"And you, Sizemore." Gibson suddenly turned to the Cardinals' woolly-haired second baseman, who was reclining against the wall a few feet away, cap lowered over closed eyes. "Tell me how you are today." It was more a challenge than an inquiry.

Sizemore, absently: "Tired."

"Tired!" bellowed Gibson. "Don't you know nearly all fatigue is psychosomatic? You ought to do something about that, Sizemore. Besides, if you didn't spend so much time screwing around in the evenings, you wouldn't be tired."

Sizemore, a family man whose swinging is confined to the batter's box, opened his eyes and grinned at Gibson. "I guess you're right," he said. "Look what it did to that thing you call a body."

Meanwhile, Fairly finished with the Dodgers and moved on to the Mets, with whom he had played during their zanier years under Casey Stengel. Stengel, Ron insisted, would spend the first day of spring training solemnly pointing out to his players that "this here, men, is the batter's box, two of them, one for right-handed batters and one for left-handed batters, and that little rise in the ground you see you there, that there is the pitcher's mound, and that's wherefrom the pitcher throws the ball at the batter."

"Bullshit, Ron," someone said. "He didn't really say that."

"He did too, I swear it," Ron twinkled. "Anyhow, some of the guys needed it. Casey had a catcher on that ballclub who always had to look down at his right hand to make sure the number of fingers he was showing his pitcher corresponded to the pitch he had in mind."

We drove back from Lakeland to St. Petersburg—Lou, his girl friend Virgie Daniels and myself. I had met her once before briefly, but this one-hour trip was the longest I'd ever spent in her company. She is a strikingly comely woman, a teacher of French in a junior high school near St. Louis. I mention her looks first not only because one normally perceives the former before learning of the latter, but also because in her case those looks are so uncommonly lovely.

She's a gentle girl too, and Lou himself is something of a pussycat when he's around her. Come to think of it, I've never seen him in anything approaching a truculent mood; he is by nature poised, easily communicative, not easily ruffled. Nevertheless, on this auto trip back from Lakeland, I sensed a warmth I hadn't noticed before in a man who ordinarily, for all his accomplished sociability, preserves a subtle kind of distance between himself and others. I can't help associating this tenderness with Virgie's presence. We talked about his children and mine, exchanging stories.

"One time," I said, "I came across my boy Luke, who was about five, sitting on the Lake Michigan beach drawing a man's head in the sand. 'That's a nice head, Luke,' I said, 'Whose is it?'

"He looked up at me, then down at the head and said simply, 'His,' pointing as if to say, 'Whose else, dummy?' "

Lou must have laughed at that for five minutes, after which he told me about his own son Lou Jr. and his girl Wanda, and how Lou Jr.—eight years old now—is capable of the same sort of condescending realism as my own son. Commented Lou: "When people say to him, 'Hey, you got the same name as your dad,' he says, 'Yeah, but I'm the one who can hit.' And he means it too. He says, 'I don't strike out very often.' "

Katie Brock divorced Lou in 1974, fourteen years after they'd said their vows. As if the winds of today's world weren't tempestuous enough to shake the foundation of any marriage, even under the most sheltered conditions, the life of a professional baseball player exerts an enormous additional stress. It is not just the unremittingly itinerant existence with all its restless, rootless anonymity that strains the bonds of any long-term close relationship, but the pressure of public exposure as well, which proffers friendship, all right, but the kind that too often turns out to be no more substantial and permanent than the newspaper the headlines are printed on.

In any event, the spring of 1975 meant a fresh start for Lou Brock on several counts: a new personal life of freedom, independence—and uncertainty—as well as a new professional season, kindredly ambiguous: marked on the one hand by the sort of renown few players ever manage to earn for themselves, and on the other, by the public demands and expectations such renown inevitably generates.

One hundred eighteen stolen bases in 1974—the all-time and quite possibly matchless record? Wonderful, sure, you bet. But that was last year. And last year, though it may have been the best year of them all for Brock, didn't grant him the most coveted prize of all, the Most Valuable Player award, which he wanted so desperately, even before the voting started. Imagine, then, how it felt once the voting was over and Lou was looking at Steve Garvey's backside, from the runnerup position.

Very simply, if you are Lou Brock you confront that question with the same equanimity and rationality—and dogged pride—with which you've confronted most of the problems of your adulthood. You encourage, as he puts it, preparation to meet opportunity.

A sense of humor touched with irony isn't out of place either. As we tooled across the causeway over Tampa Bay, in the direction of St. Pete, in the fading afternoon, Lou looked out the car window to the southwest, where the sun was heading, and said, "There's an awful lot of water out there, isn't there? And what you see is only the top."

2.
Growing Up Poor in Louisiana

Let's assume for the present, and document it as we go, that Lou Brock is everything we have so far suggested here: a spectacular athlete, of course—Hall of Fame material, and all that—as well as a man whose personal traits—intelligence, articulateness, charm and cool complexity—are just about as exceptional as his physical prowess. Let us then stack all that up against some facts of his early life: that he was one of nine children raised in the Deep South by a woman none of whose three marriages lasted long and who kept herself and her brood alive by doing field labor and domestic work.

There are some powerful contrasts in that paragraph, and they call for illumination before we go on to Brock's glory years.

How did he move from one environment to the other, in view of the spiritual light year that separates the two?

First of all, consider the odds against any such move, keeping in mind a few bare data plus the abiding condition of southern segregation, which was more than a way of life and only a little less than life itself in the sense that it shaped nearly the entire destiny of every rural or small-town black who grew up under it.

Brock's mother was bone poor when she first married and bone poor by the time her children had grown up. But she was/is clearly a decent woman, and those children returned the love she gave them. Twenty-nine years, almost three full decades, passed between the births of the first and last of her issue.

It therefore stood to reason that when they—at least the boys—finished public school, they would help her out by going to work. Or even if they didn't care to help her out, even if they moved away, they would go to work. The only common alternative to work (assuming college was uncommon) was service, which for a black youth in the middle of the twentieth century was not all that attractive. It was almost a certainty that work would consist of more of the same thing Momma had done—menial jobs or sharecropping—and that simply meant that the poverty in which she had lived her whole life would be passed on like a recessive gene to her heirs. It was a near-perfect vicious circle, and the proof of that is the fact that so few men and women ever managed to break free of it.

Lou was born in El Dorado, Arkansas, on June 18, 1939. His mother, Mrs. Paralee Brock, was lucky enough to have a midwife. She had already borne four children to a man named Sherman after whose death she met and married Maud (that's his name) Brock, by whom she had two more kids prior to Lou. After Lou she married Aaron Bell, and there were still two others from that union.

When Lou was an infant he moved with his mother to Collinston, Louisiana, a town of 300 blacks and whites. He has no childhood memories of his father, and he doesn't recall what his father did. He has in fact next to no recollections of any older males around the house, except that they were only sporadically present.

"Aaron Bell was there through five years of marriage. There were older brothers too, and two younger ones, plus husbands of older sisters, but none of them for long. People in that part of the country often just up and take off."

Didn't it bother you, I mean to have no grown man around whom you could look up to?

"Huh-uh. I wasn't used to grown males. I thought of myself as the man of the house. I got to manage my own life. Anyhow, I was preoccupied with other things that kept me from worrying about whether I had some male to identify with. Like going to school every day and wondering, am I going to be able to walk down the street today—this was Collinston; I should say 'road'—without being spat upon by a bunch of white kids on a bus. (They had the bus. We didn't.) There were good days and bad days. More good than bad. Simple pleasures; like smelling honeysuckle on the vine. I was preoccupied with everyday activities and didn't have time to wonder about segregation or grown males.

"It was really pretty simple, and yet just about everything I've ever seen since I've been in big-time baseball—all the heroics, the cowardice, the decent folks and the bums, all the shades of life—had some counterpart in Jackrabbit Junction."

What'd you call it?

"We called Doss Jackrabbit Junction, and Doss, mind you, was only a part of Collinston, where there were just 300 people to begin with, so you got to figure it was a pretty little bitty piece of earth. But when I was a kid, it held nearly everything I thought life had to offer."

Those white kids that spat at you: I suppose they got away with that pretty easily in those days, huh?

"Not on your life. We all knew who each other was, and we lived close, even if we lived apart, if you know what I mean. If I saw who it was that did that to me, I'd find him after school later

31

the same day. He knew I'd find him. Segregation made no difference."

Then what? A duel for honor?

"You can call it that. We called it a fight. We'd have it out, then many times we'd just go back to being friends again. After all, the white kid that spat at me might be the same kid I played with after school most days. With a couple of hundred people in Collinston, you didn't have much choice for playmates, regardless of your color."

Well, that sounds kind of peculiar. What about all the laws of segregation I've heard about?

"Yeah, the laws. That's just it, they were laws. I mean they were man-made. All that didn't cut much ice with kids seven or eight who were looking for something to do and somebody to do it with before they were likely to sit around comparing racial characteristics. The laws were already operating, I'm sure, and that's why the white boy had the bus and I didn't. But we didn't know about the laws until later, and when we got to be teenagers that's when things started changing.

"What I do recall was realizing, kind of gradually that the laws were artificial, that they didn't really emerge logically out of the ways things were. And since I could see how things were, I mean that the white kids functioned no differently from me or the other black kids, even if they looked different, I didn't take kindly to the laws."

There wasn't much you could do about that.

"There was more than you might think. You could prove yourself. You could say to yourself that you would do well regardless of the laws. That didn't mean breaking them, because that was out of the question. But you could stack your own dignity, pride and self-respect up against the laws, like a wall, by performing something well that no wall could keep you from performing. You did this for yourself; that way no social rules got violated. No law could strip you of these rights."

That's maybe where your taste for challenge got its start, right?

"I guess so. Hell, doesn't it make sense? If somebody else has the power to make and keep the laws, either you let them tie you up or you fight them or else you make some counter-rules for yourself. I wasn't about to be tied up, and in those days, I couldn't fight the law. But I sure as hell could set up some standards for myself and fight to retain them.

"Only remember one thing. It took a while; in fact it took a damn long while before I was conscious of what I was doing. And there were troubles along the way. Sometimes I got dumped on my butt. And even when I didn't, I had to learn how to win the right way."

"I had to learn how to pace myself." Lou laughed. "I recall my last fistfight, back in Collinston."

You mean your last fight there, or your last one ever?

"Ever. I haven't been in one since. That last one frightened me plenty. You see, by the time I was twelve I had developed a pretty fair rep as a tough kid. But I was big for my size, and I usually took on thirteen- and fourteen-year-olds. I seldom met up with other kids twelve. But there was one boy in Doss who was my age and my size, and he started giving me a hard time.

"Everybody likes a challenge! Well, we got into it, and I finally fetched him a good one, and he went down like a pole-axed steer. I mean he was out cold.

"I'd never seen anybody like that before. They threw water on him and it did no good. I was afraid I'd killed him. I can't recall ever being so scared. He finally came to, but I never tangled with anybody after that. Sometimes winning something costs you, and you have to learn that."

Seems to me you learned that by yourself, but what about those things a kid needs somebody to teach him? Didn't you miss having a father? Did you have any strong bonds, say, with neighbors?

"When I was very young, no. It was just a struggle to be a decent human being. It was enough to be alive and human; I was thankful for that. I had love from my mother and no matter what I did, I knew she gave a damn and wanted me to grow up to be respectable. That was sufficient."

So much, then, for textbook notions about father figures and

Oedipal feelings. Momma was to all appearances a strong, deeply religious, straightbacked woman whom Lou adored. His environment was as little conducive to rumination and introspection as it was demanding of self-reliance, although he does remember the loneliness of weekends, when luckier kids would all pile into a car one of their still luckier friends owned, and cruise around the neighborhood, spinning their wheels and hoping the dirt they kicked up would land on somebody. Lou would hide behind his house when he saw them coming. Kerosene lamps burned in his mother's parlor during most of his early childhood, and he recalls the wonder of seeing his first electric light. Still later, there was TV—he was about eleven—but in somebody's else's place, of course. He would walk a mile or two now and then to the house of some family with a set. They would watch the fights together. Or he might tag along with Willie Daniel, of a Sunday morning, when Willie normally went to a nearby field to break in horses.

Sometimes they would watch the baseball game of the week, but baseball did not interest him. During his early life he never played it, never had a ball thrown to him, never caught one. Then one day when he was nine, he did, under unusual circumstances.

"You have to understand," he said, reflecting on it later, "that I had one big advantage when I was a kid. My mother was high on education. So was our preacher. So was my teacher. Until I was twelve, I went to school in a shack with no running water, with one room, and that one teacher and sixty kids strung out over six grades. There was no way she could keep that mob in line except with a hard hand.

"She came to live at our house when I was nine. As I remember it, Momma let us know it was very important to have somebody around who was educated. The teacher—great name she had too, Sophronia Young—was all the time telling us to pay attention to the world outside, to the people—that means the blacks—who had gone on and done something with themselves, far away from wherever they came from. She hated to see us waste our time. She said, 'Read newspapers, listen to the radio. Learn something so you won't end up baling hay.'

"Anyhow, one day in class I had found a rubberband, so I shaped a very fine spitball for it. And there was a little girl right in front of me who I decided to fire the spitball at. And just at the moment I fired, she ducked, and the spitball caught Miss Young right behind the ear.

"You can believe she was mad. At that time they could take the strap and put it to you, but she had another punishment in mind for me. She told me to go to what she called 'the Library'— it was nothing but a little bookstand in the corner of the schoolroom—and look up four or five ballplayers—Jackie Robinson, Campanella, Newcombe, Joe DiMaggio and Stan Musial, I can still remember them. Then I was to stand before that class, with all the six grades in it, and give a report on what I'd read.

"I was in fourth grade. I'd hardly ever even heard of baseball. Believe me, there was no worse punishment she could have thought up.

"And there was more to it. She told me to go out on the softball field and play first base in a softball game. I'd never been out there before. And every time I'd drop a ball that was thrown to me, I'd get five licks on the hand."

With . . .?

"That strap. And because she lived with us, she did not take pity."

She gave you the licks?

"Oh yeah. And I took it. I knew I'd get a whipping anyway when I got home, 'cause she'd tell my mom.

"Anyway, from reading all those books on those players, I saw somewhere that they got, mind you, eight dollars a day in meal money. *Eight dollars a day in meal money* . . . now what in the world, I said to myself, were they making a *week*?"

So Lou Brock grew up with no man at his side, or so he claims: only a strong mother and, for a time, a strong bachelor lady grade-school teacher who literally whipped him into catching a softball for the first time.

But the very notion of a singular male model—a father or its equivalent—may just be a middle-class notion. Huck Finn would agree. For Lou had plenty of males around him, after all. The more he talks about this the more evident it becomes that his upbringing had much of the tribal about it. There were packs of young men in Collinston in their twenties and thirties who would come swinging past his house on their way somewhere, maybe a sandlot ballgame. They would speak to him—one of them in particular would, a man named Noah Pates—and say, "Hi, buddy!" and Lou, with all the worshipful passion a twelve-year-old boy can feel for a twenty-four-year-old man who cares enough to say hello to him, would holler, "Hey, lemme go with ya!"

Noah always let him go. Noah was what Lou's momma called decent, and she figured if Lou went with Noah to watch him play ball, he had to be in good hands.

Then one day Noah stuck Lou in the outfield, deep in the outfield, during a practice batting session. "You just throw the balls back that we hit out there," he said. "But don't try to catch 'em or get in their way. Let 'em roll dead. I don't want you gettin' hurt." This advice, if you please, to Louis Clark Brock, who, sixteen years later, hit .464 in the World Series and drove the Detroit Tigers to distraction.

So at last a fly ball stopped a few feet away from Lou, who picked it up and winged a perfect strike to home plate.

"Hey!" yelled Pates or somebody (it could have been anybody). "Can you throw like that all the time?"

"Uh-huh. I think so."

"Can you hit?"

"Yes, I think so."

"Well, try it. Come on in here. Pick up a bat and try hittin' one or two."

So he tried hitting one or two and both of them sailed over the rightfielder's head, rolling dead before anyone got to them.

The talent had bloomed. It bloomed pretty late and rather by accident, especially if you think about it relative to the devices for manufacturing prodigies that are practiced by today's Little League parents. But once it came, it hung on. Lou was fourteen and a freshman in Union High School in nearby Mer Rouge when he tried out for the one opening—a pitcher's spot—that was left on the seventeen-man school squad. He won it by the simple (and again, very un-Little Leaguelike) expedient of throwing a baseball farther than any of his dozen or so coauditioners.

Repeat, a baseball. Up until then it had been all softball for him, but things were happening fast now, the way the adolescent juices run, and on the opening day of the 1954 season, Lou Brock was the starting pitcher for Union, batting in the cleanup position. He had reached his full height of five feet ten inches and he weighed 165, three pounds lighter than he is today. Not bad for a kid who five years earlier aimed a spitball at a little girl less than a yard in front of him and missed.

His batting average during his senior year wasn't bad either: .540. By now Mrs. Paralee Brock's fourth boychild was Slugger Brock, and thinking the thoughts any young black might whose natural advantages were meager in most respects and rich in maybe only a couple, intelligence and a talent for athletics. He kept watching the mail for some sign of interest from a major-league scout, or at least from a college or university that might be eager to recruit a .540 high school walloper for its incoming class.

Nothing. No letter; no postcard. Collinston might as well have been in Outer Mongolia for all the attention the Slugger was attracting. Suddenly upon graduation, his options were fewer, the implacable realities of adult life in the black South closer than he had ever consciously envisioned. Now it was either the big push that Momma, the preacher and the lady teacher had been talking about: college—most likely with nobody's help—or else—well, or else what?

It took him four days to find out what for certain. He didn't really require that much; he already knew what was about to be demonstrated to him. But the young squander time, and proof comes slowly to them. So despite the fact that he and his nephew Harvey were bright enough to finish third and first, respectively, in their 1957 graduating class of 105, the two of them decided to take a summer job baling hay. Postgraduate education, you might say—and say it with a straight face—for the two of them found out on Thursday after starting on Monday that "overtime" was a concept they must have picked up from one of those alien sources like television or the newspapers that his teacher had talked about. Down here, where the hay was, there was just so much of it to bale each day, and that's what you drew your pay for, regardless of how much time it took you. It took Lou and Harvey sixteen hours on every one of those four days.

By the Saturday after that Thursday they were on the campus of Southern University in Baton Rouge, having been driven there by an alumnus, one of their high school instructors, a man who had long endeavored to sell the idea of college to both of them. Lou had $6 in his pocket and no place to spend the night. The administrative offices of the university were closed for the weekend.

To these little miseries I might add the obvious: that he had left his mother to shift for herself back in Collinston. Yet by now, with the smell of the hay still on his clothes, he knew, with a bitter, newly refined certainty, that he could be of no substantial help to her by simply taking a place at her side in the fields for the rest of their life together. At the worst, college would be a quick failure; at best, the planation was a slow one.

Lou made his way to the university's physical plant that day and finding it open, managed to sign on for yard work and a bed in a nearby military barracks. Harvey got a cashier clerk's job at the YMCA. He was a bit smaller than Lou and also knew how to work a cash register. The two boys were admitted to the freshman class three months later. They even obtained some financial aid on the strength of their high school grade averages. Now the game was for keeps.

Freshman year, the first away from home, was no triumph, either academically or athletically. In fact it was more like a chain of juvenile mistakes that came close to strangling him in both those phases of his life. First his grades fell off—the not uncommon Freshman Slump—which resulted in the loss of his partial scholarship, which led him to attempt the baseball route, which prompted him to ask for a two-week leave from his grass-cutting job in order to try out for the team.

His reasoning made sense on the face of it: A solid assignment on the team might yield an athletic scholarship and the chance to continue his education. But this wasn't Collinston, it was Baton Rouge, Big Town ("They had electric street lights there, man!") and Southern University was not Union High School. The student body, though mostly Southern, came from all over the United States. Noah Pates seemed long gone. The one upperclassman Lou approached to give him a hand as he tried to make the team—a New Orleans senior named Mel Carriere—had troubles of his own staying on the roster, and he was not about to be any gangling freshman's crutch.

So there was Brock, the pride of Union High School, consigned to the Siberia of the outfield and shagging flies again, this time with nobody around to see to it he wasn't bopped by any of them. There he stayed for a week, two weeks, never getting close to a turn at bat and never even catching the ear, needless to say the eye, of a coach who already had more talent on his squad than he needed.

Three weeks turned into four, and Lou lost his job on top of his scholarship. He lost, in fact, another thing: one day, quite literally, his sensibility. In the middle of a long practice session spent racing all over the outfield in a desperate effort to run down everything hit in any direction, he simply passed out cold, collapsed in a sweaty little heap on the Louisiana grass, unconscious from sheer exhaustion.

When he came around, the coaches Bob Lee and Emory Hines, were talking to him for the first time, jollying him along in tones meant to soothe him but likewise to get him to forget this foolishness and go back wherever he came from. "Tell you what," the man said. "Why don't you grab a bat when you feel up to it. We'll let you have a crack at four or five pitches. O.K.?"

Four or five pitches! After a month of beating my head against the wall out here!? Noah, baby, where are you now that I need you?

Noah, come to think of it, *was* there, if you know that I mean. So was Momma and so was the bachelor lady grade-school teacher, plus Roy Campanella and Jackie Robinson. Lou picked up a bat, the bees still buzzing furiously in his head, squared off against the pitcher (it was Carriere!), and hit every one of the five pitches over the right-field fence.

Now look at that coach's face! Listen to him ask my name, and where I come from and what position I favor and would I like to come back tomorrow and suit up? And listen to me say right back at him yes*sir*, I most certainly would and will. . . .

Let us duck the rest of that freshman year. It is all anticlimax, with not an iota more of Frank Merriwell about it. Brock stayed with the team all right, but he hit .140 for the season and struck out so often, he remembers, that "I kept the air around home plate cool."

Sophomore year was another matter, markedly more attractive to record. Lou set a conference record for hitting that still stands (.545, compounded of eighty hits and thirteen home runs in 27 games), and Southern became the first black college to win the NAIA baseball championship. Now at last, here they came, in breathless droves: the big-league scouts, so long desired, so long neglectful, but at this golden moment all full of good cheer and enterprise. And as they gathered around, a letter arrived from the United States Olympic Committee inviting Lou to be a member of the American baseball team in the 1959 Pan-American Games in Chicago.

That last one was too good to miss. Lou was still a college kid, not out of his teens, and the Games represented just about the highest honor an amateur baseball player could aspire to. Pro ball could wait at least until they were over.

Besides, they meant climbing on an airplane for the first time in his life and traveling, at somebody else's expense, to a city 1,000 miles away that, believe it or not, was not only bigger but *much* bigger than Baton Rouge. Think of the street lights *there*. If only he had realized that the meal on the menu the stewardess showed him was a free meal and not something so costly it didn't even have a price on it, he would surely have ordered some. He was pretty hungry by the time he got to Chicago.

And weary to boot, when he finished taking several buses and an El train (taxis were for the rich) to the athletes' quarters at the University of Chicago. He arrived with two heavy suitcases and exactly twice as much money—$12—as he had when he'd first seen Baton Rouge two years before. He looked like a rumpled black rube.

"Hey, man, you a boxer?" a voice chirped behind him. He turned to face a slicked-up, caramel-colored teenager, maybe a couple of years younger than himself, but obviously one of his teammates. The boy flashed him a smirk that looked like a contemputous smirk and feinted a punch at him.

"No," was all Lou could think to say.

"And you sure as hell don't look up to bein' one," said Caramel Face, who smirked and giggled and feinted some more, than danced down the hall away from him.

Today Lou says he was all set to take that kid on ("Hell, he wasn't any bigger than me"), but the kid was gone by the time Lou set his bags down. "That kid turned out to be Muhammad Ali, and at that moment I didn't like him. They called him Cassius Clay then, but he hasn't changed his verbal style much since. He got a good deal bigger though. Maybe it's just as well I didn't untangle myself from those bags any quicker than I did."

Twenty years old at the time, Lou couldn't even drive a car; he'd never had the chance. The impression forms that Bob Gibson's remarks years later in the St. Petersburg clubhouse—about the hay in Lou's hair—had a basis in fact. But it is equally apparent from all we've added, that Brock was

41

nothing if not a quick study. The hay got combed out fast
enough. If the seventeen-year-old Cassius Clay made him look a
little dumb in that Chicago dormitory hallway, he rebounded
well. By the time the Pan-Am Games were over, he and a couple
of other youngsters he quickly made friends with, named Oscar
Robertson and Jerry West, were running life at a pretty fast clip in
the big city.

Running. Sooner or later you get around to that. Brock was
swift from the start, as far back as prebaseball days when he was a
proud little twelve-year-old tough kid and Sugar Ray Robinson
meant vastly more to him than Robinson or Campanella. But he
reminds you: "All the kids in Collinston were fast. I was no
exception." All the kids everywhere; speed is cheap. By the time
he was competing in Chicago with the best amateur talent in the
Western Hemisphere, he knew he had to figure quite a few things
out in his head, to add to whatever natural talent he possessed, if
he was to make anything of himself in the games he played.

Here again one discerns the imprint of Mother Brock,
and all that business about growing up Respectable. But a lot
of the adult Lou Brock himself is there: the tireless observer,
the cool but compulsive analyst, the player sportswriters say talks
about stealing bases with the vocabulary and mental set of a
professor. They are right about him. It took him 3.2 seconds to
steal off Wilbur Wood, a calculation that is his, not mine, and
based on a lot of empirical reckoning. At Southern he majored for
a time in architecture, than switched to mathematics. (His
grades, by the way, improved dramatically after that cockeyed
first year.) He has something approaching total recall, a gift which
he takes pains to distinguish from mere good memory. "I didn't
understand chemistry really, but I got respectable grades in it
because I could close my eyes during exams and perceive every
formula I ever saw written on the blackboard."

In retrospect, then, the most important acquaintance he
made at the Pan-Am Games was a young runner named Deacon
Jones, as bright in his own right as Lou, a guy who has in the
meantime become Lou's best and most abiding friend.

Deacon taught Lou some things about running, or more

properly, Lou learned them from Deacon, by watching him on
the track, taking off from the blocks, accelerating, hitting full
stride. Lou studied Deacon day after day and decided there were
important things a ballplayer could learn from a sprinter. He filed
what he saw, stashed it away in his head, where it stayed securely,
waiting to be utilized at some later date.

The very concept of the later date prompted him to ignore
the offers of the major-league scouts and return to Southern
following the Games. He still had two years of school and too
much to learn, not just about a game he had begun to play there,
but from the people who had begun to teach it to him. And for all
that racing around big, kaleidoscopic Chicago, the exhilarating
variety of people he had met there, the taste of sports at the top
competitive level, and the adulation it inspires—for all that, the
classrooms of Baton Rouge maintained first priority in his scheme
of things. He remembered the hay-baling and the spitting white
kids, not to mention his mother's voice. The important thing was
to escape the plantation, by whatever Respectable means, and
even as late as the fall of 1959, the degree from Southern
University seemed the most reliable way, if not the most
glamorous. In some respects Lou Brock is not fast but slow, as
deliberate as a cat lying in wait.

Nevertheless, he was also a kid not yet of legal age. The
Games did change things unalterably, despite all his ongoing
academic resolve, and certainly enough to make his junior year
measurably different from that spectacular sophomore romp.
There is nothing wrong with the .370 average he posted during
his third college season, but it is not the stuff of which scouts'
dreams are made. So while they kept their eyes on Lou Brock,
those eyes were not altogether so misty as before.

From this information one begins to pick up more signals
from Brock's psyche. The greater the competitive pressure, the
more likely he is to excel, which helps to explain why he is one of
the great clutch players of contemporary baseball. It is the
when-preparation-meets-opportunity pattern he loves to lecture
you on. Conversely—and self-analyst that he is, he admits it with
a degree of rue—one of his chief weaknesses is the inability to

perform when the challenge is wanting. Statistics, he says, can be cited to prove this.

In any case, I am affirming now that he dropped to .370 during his junior year partly because baseball at Southern University was less of a challenge then than it had been a year earlier. If tailing off to .370 is stretching a point, it is Lou Brock who makes the point. In turn if it is he who is stretching it, the fact remains he finally did quit Southern at the outset of his senior year, mainly because he could not concentrate on his studies. During the summer of 1960, following junior season, he had returned to Chicago and tried out with both the Cubs and White Sox. He garnered offers from each team, and decided the one the Cubs made sounded pretty good. Several other clubs —Milwaukee, Los Angeles, Baltimore—were eyeing him at the time, but they were uniformly well-stocked with outfielders, while the Cubs were in the midst of one of their seemingly perpetual rebuilding campaigns. The best chance seemed to be in Chicago. He kept coming back to Chicago.

In short, he had a lot rattling around in his head when he returned to Baton Rouge for one last try at the bachelor's degree. And if the problem of turning pro wasn't enough to disturb the concentration usually required in senior year, there was an additional little item named Katie Hay.

Maybe it's another measure of Brock's pious upbringing—a life that sounds as if it belonged to America of the 1910s rather than the 1940s and 1950s—that we have had so little to say about his young way with women. Some way. He missed the girl with the spitball at age nine—that we've already established—and it took him quite a while before he ever got significantly closer.

Along the way he groped. In high school as late as the eleventh grade, he recalls, girls were something you occasionally did homework with, in which case the only difference between them and boys was that you acted a good deal more asininely around them. "Oh, I knew there was something more to them," he says. "Of *course* I knew it. All that dumbass horsing around was a sign I knew it very painfully. But I thought there was a prescribed way of Talking With Girls, and I sure as hell didn't know what it was, but it certainly was frightening.

And I wasn't really that much different from anyone else around me.

"I tried, I tried hard. All of us tried hard. But God, we were such jackasses! I recall several times a bunch of guys wanted to spike the punch at some party so that they could get the girls there high and make out. But they'd invariably test the punch beforehand and get so loaded themselves they couldn't even begin to talk to them."

In that kind of backwoods America, more firmly than long dead, it was standard to marry when you were still up to your eyeballs in sexual innocence . . . boys no less than girls. Equally standard was the sanction and encouragement of the adult world. Ashford Williams, high school counselor, and devoted baseball fan, often talked to Lou. Marriage, said Williams, is better before a pro career begins than after it is established. "You'll meet too many people too casually by the time you're at the top," Ashford emphasized. "And *you're* going to be at the top. You get my meaning, I'm sure: Marry now, or you'll never know what love is."

If the advice sounds touchingly antiquated today, it made sense to Lou then. Indeed he still thinks there's a melancholy truth to it. In any event, less than a month after he started his senior year, he decided there was no coping with Southern anymore. The next phase of his life had become as irresistible as it had become clear. He decided to accept the $30,000 bonus the Cubs had offered him. So he went up to Chicago to sign his contract, and while he was there he was issued a portion of his first salary as a professional athlete.

It was a check, obviously, and just as obviously, checks are meant to be cashed, right? He knew that much; he wasn't born yesterday. So he found a currency exchange in the Loop, where he gave the teller the check and the teller handed him a pack of bills coming to $4,500 in cash.

Mr. Sophistication. Lou spent about five minutes staring at the money, turning it over in his hands, counting it, recounting it. He had never had more than $20 on his person at any one time before.

"That teller must have thought I was nuts," he said later. "Or more likely, and he would have been right, that I'd just crawled out of the bayou for my first natural-born look at the daylight."

The cash was mostly in tens and twenties, since he knew, or since he thought, that when he got back to Southern to pack his things he might have had a hard time changing as much as a fifty. So he stuffed the heap of greenbacks into every pocket of his clothing ("I looked like a sack of pool balls") and walked over to the Greyhound station to catch a bus for Baton Rouge. Lou Brock, with $4,500 literally bristling from him, on a bus headed for the Southland and a date with destiny. He made it back to Louisiana weary but unrobbed—thanks more to fate than foresight—and proceeded to make preparations for a bigger journey: out to Arizona and an assignment in the Instructional League. Shortly before Christmas of that year, 1960, he and Katie Hay swore eternal and official fidelity to each other.

3. Success in the Minors— Then Chicago

Lou Brock during his early professional career was a curious compound of swaggering self-assurance and gnawing anxiety. It stands to reason. His entire life until then had consisted of a struggle between the little he had been given and the lot he yearned to get. Reality fought constantly with desire, circumstance with possibility.

He was Pore Boy to the manner born, a sharecropper's kid from the piney woods who suffered from the ignorance and tunnel vision that go with poverty. Still, he had a clearheaded mother and close ties with his tribe, not to mention several striking native gifts of his own that were fired by a fierce urge to rise above the poverty. With a mixed pedigree like that, he was one part tiger

47

cub, one part rabbit. What we have said so far bears this out. So does what follows.

To begin with, he performed handsomely in the Instructional League. There, during the fall and early winter of 1960–61, he played in about forty games against talent that ranged in caliber from major league down to Class A. They had been brought together to help them gain some special strength they had been lacking in.

Brock's lack was fundamentally experience. The natural ability was in him, the challenge was in the league and—perhaps I should say so—he batted .387 for the time he was there. The Chicago Cubs promptly summoned him to 1961 spring training in Mesa, where he took part in another several dozen games and turned in a sizzling .400 mark.

All this stood for Brock the tiger. The rabbit, meanwhile, crouched inside him. Even as he was playing well in Arizona, he kept hearing the phrase—and it kept eating away at him—"Wait till the bell rings!"

In other words, just wait, hotshot, until your opposition *really* turns it on against you, until they commence being serious. Then maybe you won't look like such a dude. Up till now they've been practicing. Don't jump to any conclusions about your immortality.

So on the one hand Brock felt insulted, dealt a raw deal, when the Cubs shipped him off to St. Cloud, Minnesota, a Class C club, for the 1961 season. "Class C is just one step up from the bottom," he moped. "And fully five rungs from the top. The Cubs know how well I hit in the Instructional League and spring training in Mesa—against damn good opposition too, sure as hell better than Class C."

On the other hand, spake the rabbit: "What this must mean is that they weren't kidding about that bell ringing. They haven't really thrown their best stuff at me. They must know, better than I do, that when they feel like it, they'll tie me in knots."

The question arises: How close in motivation is anxiety to challenge? Evidently close enough in some people for the distinction to blur at a certain point—which was reached for Lou in his first trip to the plate at St. Cloud.

He remembers three sensations: shivering from fear, then hitting the first pitch out of the ballpark, then shivering again as he rounded the bases, this time from a surge of confidence that mingled with an almost transcendent sense of relief.

The scenario sounds repetitive. What he had done at age fourteen against the pitching of Noah Pates' buddies, and at age eighteen against Mel Carriere at Southern, he was doing again here in St. Cloud.

The tiger cub took over from the rabbit for almost but not quite all of the remainder of the year. In August Brock was leading the league with a .400 batting average. Well, said the Cubs, let's give this phenom a look: Come on down to Chicago, Lou; we'll put you out in the garden for a few licks at the end of the season.

Brock's bat broke into a cold sweat. By the end of the regular Northern League campaign his average had dropped fully forty points. At .361 that was still good enough to lead the league. So were his totals of runs scored (117), hits (181), doubles (33) and putouts (277). He also stole 38 bases.

I might add he had the requisite courage to show up at Wrigley Field in September. But it was clearly going to take time to grow up.

Katie Brock was a dietitian, and a good one, product of the same Union High School where she had first met Lou, and of Southern University, where their courtship had unfolded. She was as serious about her calling as he was about his, and when she got an offer to intern at Indiana University about the same time Lou was sent off to St. Cloud, she figured she couldn't turn it down. The result of this was a suitcase marriage in the early years, with hopes for something better later on. For now she would do what she could to hike up to Minnesota whenever possible and join Lou for a few days in the apartment he had rented from a German couple who were remarkably cordial toward the black athletes they were still unaccustomed to seeing in the uniform of blue-eyed St. Cloud.

But she brought paperwork with her, on which she was

obliged to labor often until late at night, past the time Lou
went to bed to pick up the sleep his own livelihood demanded.
"I had to devote all my energies to making the big leagues. I even
ate all my meals with the people I roomed with. I was a college
man and most of my teammates were very young so there weren't
many common interests. It was an existence that had really only
one facet: a single-minded devotion to realizing my dream at
becoming a major leaguer. That's what I felt it would take and I
was very serious about it.

Brock came to Chicago with a fair lot of hot press going for him.
You can imagine it. The Cubs were starving for success. They
hadn't won a pennant in seventeen years, and whatever merit
they possessed as a team was associated with raw batting power,
not with speed or with pitching. Ernie Banks, Ron Santo, Billy
Williams: That was it, that was just about all the Cubs could put
together in the way of a weapon.

But look now: A bright young black prize has come along
name of Lou Brock, with not only a reputation as a long-ball
hitter, which fits the Cubs' image, such as it is, but who can fly,
which doesn't, and which surely has to add a dimension badly
missing around here for a long time. Look at his credentials while
you're at it, those averages in college, Instructional League, St.
Cloud . . . pretty terrific. Why, you know he slammed a home
run out in Mesa this spring that was measured at over 480 feet?
The only other guy that ever hit one that far out there was Ted
Williams. But it's not just power, it's speed. He makes it to first
base in 3.4 seconds on a full swing and 3.1 on a drag bunt. Can't
you just see him doing that in Wrigley Field? Why, people in
Chicago aren't even used to *looking* that fast. . . .

Lou read the papers as well as the next man, and what he saw
might well have reinforced the confidence his St. Cloud year had
instilled in him. But it didn't; the rabbit woke up. Quite frankly,
he had a terrible time.

You can read it in the stats. He hit .263 in 1962 and stole
sixteen bases. He dropped to .258 the following season and stole

24. Twenty-four bases is not bad, especially in Chicago, a city where it is taken for granted that everybody steals but the Cubs. Still, Brock was supposed to be jet-propelled. The previous year, 1962, the Dodgers' Maury Wills had picked up 104 bases, an all-time record. Maybe you don't expect anything quite like that from a second-year man, but 24? And how many times did he get gunned down?

The performance was hardly what Brock or anybody else had in mind. Figures aside, his vulnerability was evident in his personal demeanor. I have to remind you here that I know him today as a natural and rather wonderfully charming breeze-shooter with the most infectious laugh I have ever heard out of a man. He is ease incarnate.

In Chicago in 1962 he was pure overwound rigidity. He did not chat with his teammates, in the dugout or out. He bumbled constantly at the bat, in the field ("he hand-fought ground balls," one reporter said), on the basepaths, he—well, here's his own pitching teammate Larry Jackson on the subject:

"He'd break out in a big sweat just putting on his uniform. His desire was so intense that he made things tough for himself. He didn't know when to slide and was so fast that, before he realized it, he tore the bag right out of the ground."

A writer on the *Chicago Daily News* called him a butcher, even as late as April of 1963. "If you have watched all the Cub home games thus far," Bob Smith remarked, "you probably have come to the conclusion that Lou Brock is the worst outfielder in baseball history. He really isn't, but he hasn't done much to prove it."

"Well," says Lou, from the perspective of his present thirty-seven years, "that's putting at a mite harshly. But not altogether wrongly. I was bad news. I had trouble with ground balls but I could throw. I also had difficulties with lefthanders. The coaches would get me out to Wrigley Field at 8 A.M. every day, practice all morning long and then—after all that—I'd have nothing left for the game. It was kind of sad to do all that work and have nothing left for the game.

"But if I may say so, the Cubs lost 110 games in 1962. I'm not sure I saw anybody on the team lose all that victoriously.

"Besides, if this shows something about me, it also shows
something about the difference between the big leagues and the
minors. In St. Cloud, for instance, I played almost nothing but
night ball. Now, suddenly, I was in Wrigley Field, where they
have no lights, and it's a little late to be learning about sunglasses,
right? Here comes a fly ball, and I got these glasses on that I don't
know when to flip. If I flip them too late I can't see the ball. If I flip
them too soon I can't see the ball. I think that's when people
started saying, 'Where are you now, Joe DiMaggio.' "

At the same time, during those two dolorous years with the
Cubs, Brock suffered as much from psychological as from
technical malfunction. Admittedly, that is normal for any rookie,
and rookie Brock reacted normally—that is, with the expectable
degree of paralyzed awe when he first entered the Wrigley Field
clubhouse and was assigned a locker. But what was not par, for
any young or even old player, in fact what remains one of the
weirder chapters in the managerial history of major-league
baseball, was the system by which the Cub team was run at the
time Brock joined it.

It had no manager. It had fourteen managers, or "coaches,"
as they were called, who shared authority equally.

What name would you give such an arrangement? If
government by three leaders is a triumvirate (in ancient Rome a
notoriously inefficient political form), did the Cubs have a
quattuordecimvirate? If the question is silly, it has that much in
common with the Chicago system itself, which the Cubs' fey
chewing-gum magnate-owner P. K. Wrigley instituted one day in
1961, possibly after he had run out of patience with his bumbling
team.

As matters were organized, one coach would be head
coach—in effect, manager—for a preordained period of two
weeks, followed by another coach for a similar span, then
another, until all fourteen had had their crack at the money. Then
around again. In the course of this, rules, regulations, policies
and habits sometimes changed like slides in an old stereopticon,
leaving a confused after-image in the eyes of the ballplayers.
Fourteen coaches would hover constantly, thirteen of whom
were responsible to one other. The responsibility was always

temporary, however, a condition which caused the one to be insecure in his authority and the others to be officious in theirs. "Fourteen chiefs," said Lou Brock, "is an awful lot of brass for just 25 Indians, only eight of whom play everyday anyhow. The system was not good for morale, and there was plenty of tendency toward insubordination on the team. The trouble was, how could you know who to be insubordinate to?"

And how could a very young player begin to develop a sense of what he could do or could not do?

Coach A: Pull the ball.

Coach B: I wouldn't pull the ball that way, kid, if I was you: learn to place it.

Coach C: Hey, Brock, why are you trying so hard to pull the ball one minute and place it the next? Relax! Do what comes naturally!

Coach D: Where's your head, kid? Bear down! Pay some attention to what you're doing!

Coach E: Bunt, baby, bunt!

Brock began to feel like one of Pavlov's experimental dogs, those poor beasts the old Russian psychologist used to drive a little nuts by mixing up the correlation between bells ringing and food rewarded, between stimulus, that is, and response. Some of the instruction Lou got helped, no doubt—like Coach Charlie Metro's observation one day that the distance between first and second base is not ninety feet but rather the number of steps you could make it in fastest. "In your case, Lou," said Metro, "thirteen." Brock didn't see the usefulness of that at the time, but later, like the things he had perceived in a more confident day from watching Deacon Jones run, the knowledge was put to use.

For now, however, that grim couple of years in Chicago, he was a troubled youngster. And since we are talking so much in psychological terms, it might just be that some patterns in the eventual psychotherapeutic salvation of Lou Brock do become apparent in the reminiscences most vivid in his mind today.

He relishes what he learned from Ernie Banks, the magnificent hitter of home runs. Banks, of course, was Mr. Cub, the single player in the otherwise lusterless Chicago organization who owned and fully deserved superstar status in those days, moreover, one of the most dedicated, unswerving, twelve-cylinder optimists the game has ever known. In addition to these traits, which everyone knows about, he was, Lou remembers, a great and soothing simplifier of issues.

He would lay his homilies on Lou at all hours (the two men were roommates): "When you walk up to the plate," Ernie would muse, "there's really only three factors involved: you, the pitcher and the ball. Once the ball is released, there's only two factors: you and the ball. And hell, Lou, the ball is just a round, hard piece of horsehide, but *you* are a man with a bat in your hands and good eyes in your head. So whaddya mean, you can't hit Koufax?"

Lou would blink at this pretty little sophistry, but he liked it. It put him at ease, if only for a moment, and ease was exactly what did not come easily. Bob Kennedy knew it too. Kennedy was the man who in 1963 finally emerged from the chaos of the fourteen scurrying Keystone Cops into the position of head coach of the Cubs. (The oldest continuous franchise in the major leagues was still so infatuated with collegiate nomenclature that it couldn't bring itself to call Kennedy by his professional name, a manager.)

Anyhow, the team was lounging around the clubhouse in Cincinnati one afternoon, waiting for the start of a game delayed by rain. Suddenly Kennedy, who was sitting by himself in a far corner, called Brock over to him. He had been brooding about his young charge, so obviously gifted, so clearly failing in the realization of his gifts.

"Write your signature here," he said, shoving a blank sheet of paper at Brock, who did so quickly, if with some mystification (he was used to quick compliance with mystifying instructions).

"No. Write it again," said Kennedy. "This time slowly. Think about every letter. Write each one of them very carefully."

Compliance again.

"Now look at the difference," said Kennedy. "I bet you couldn't even get your bank to pass that second signature. It doesn't look anywhere like your handwriting.

"What you did was, you let your conscious take over from

your subconscious on that second try. That's why it looks unlike you. And that's what you do all the time at the plate, my friend. If ever I saw a self-conscious baseball player with his brains tied in a knot, it's you. You are forever thinking about whether your stance is right, whether your shoulders are balanced, whether you're swinging correctly. Tell you one thing: You squeeze that bat so hard, sometimes I think I see sawdust coming out of the handle. Now you know you didn't do that at St. Cloud."

Kennedy was right, although Banks had said the same thing with more charm, more amiably. So Brock remembered it longer from Ernie. Anyhow, the upshot of both messages was that Lou was thinking too much about the game and playing it too little. Yet I have said that he still thinks today, in fact that a perpetual tendency toward self-analysis is imprinted in him. I haven't needed to lean on the fact that he now plays like a sonofabitch. The question then is how he got all the contradictions untangled.

The fact is, he did it the way anybody else would do it—in moments, occasions and flashes, with disheartening stretches of languor in between. The progress looks gradual only from a distance. Up close it was a matter of single events, like that storied monster of a home run in New York.

Twice on that day in June, 1962, he came up, and twice he whiffed. Under the circumstances it was a little hard to remember any successes. Indeed there was only one thing on his mind in the fifth inning, when he took his place at the plate against Al Jackson. For God's sake let me hit one, even if it's a pop to the pitcher. Let me just get some wood on it. Let me. . . .

Jackson's pitch was a curve that came soaring in at about the level of the *C* on Brock's cap. Moreover, it was outside, a perfectly third-rate throw, the kind only an uncertain hitter might ever swing at.

Brock offered. Better to say he chopped, took a violent downswing, no thing of beauty, though he recognized quickly enough that the fly ball it produced had rather considerable potential for distance. The ball was hit to dead center. Lou took off like a shot. There might be a triple in this one, he reckoned, if Richie Ashburn can't catch up with it.

Better than that! was his next realization, for there was

umpire Tom Gorman flashing him the home-run sign. Four bases! What Gorman must mean (what else could he mean??) is that I got a chance for an inside-the-park home run . . . that wall is all of 483 feet away . . . if the ball rolls that far I can beat Ashburn's throw . . . that's got to be what Gorman is telling me.

Brock let the throttle out. Twenty-two years old and for all his troubles as fast as any player alive, he moved so swiftly he didn't even have to slide into home plate, for he had already seen that the Mets' catcher was just standing there. Ashburn's throw was obviously too late.

In fact, now he saw that everybody was just standing there, unmoving, looking out toward center field. Funny. He trotted into the dugout, expecting handshakes all around. Funnier still. Everybody in the dugout was standing there, also unmoving, staring.

Somebody must have realized, probably from observing the unnecessary haste with which he circled the bases, that Brock didn't know he had hit the ball over the wall into dead center field.

"Do you know where that thing went, Lou?"

Lou turned and glanced out to center field, where Ashburn was still looking up into the bleachers, a picture of incredulity.

"There? Into the seats?"

Yes, there, in the Polo Grounds, Circus Maximus of ballparks, just a foot or two to the right of the straightaway center field 483-foot mark, where nobody had ever hit a baseball before in championship play. To left-center and right-center, 460 feet away, yes, it had been done: by Ruth, who kissed a pair there in 1921, and by Joe Adcock, who hit one in 1953. Luke Easter made it to right-center in a Negro league game once. But this was the moment of the deflowering of dead center. For what it's worth, next day they decided to tear the Polo Grounds down.

Brock's response to all this was ecstatic bewilderment. Character, as I say, develops in arrhythmic stops and starts, and right now, oddly enough, he was thinking thoughts that were probably less healthy for him than a quiet welling up of self-confidence.

Yeah! I guess maybe I am a slugger.

Well, Brock was no slugger—we may as well affirm that now—leastwise not the kind that hits home runs often, which is the only kind worthy of the name or capable of profiting from the special concentration a pull hitter needs to apply to his chores.

Another, perhaps, more seminal incident occurred in May of 1964. The Reds are in town. Enough of the season has been played already to have nudged the Cubs uneasily closer to the judgment that their young prize from St. Cloud was not going to live up to all his evidently golden promise. The desperation was growing within Lou himself. Now and then he would think back to the warning he first heard in Arizona—"Wait till the bell rings"—whereupon he would flirt seriously with the conclusion that it had already rung for him, as early as April of 1962 when the major-leaguers started throwing at him in earnest. Now he was getting ready to be carted out of the ring, with defeat all over his face. When he had listened to Ashford Williams' advice to marry young, he had also vowed to follow the older man's suggestion that he allot three years to pro ball before giving up on it or himself. It was already past the deadline.

In fact within just a few weeks the Cubs themselves would give up on him and he would be traded off to St. Louis. Between now and then, however, this moment in May and that one in June, Vada Pinson hit a savage clothesliner into the right-center-field district of Wrigley Field that changed Lou Brock's mind even if it didn't substantially affect the thinking of the Cubs.

It was a screamer, with only a couple of feet of arch to its trajectory, the perfect high-off-the-wall double. Brock even figured it was headed for the seats. He went up for it; not to catch it but to show he tried.

He caught it, but he may have been the last man in the park to know he did. He recalls crashing to the ground, feeling "as though my teeth would fly out of my mouth," getting up painfully but reflexively, looking around for the ball, not seeing it anywhere, panicking, then, Sweet Jesus, finding it in the webbing of his glove, a discovery that was the only way of explaining all the fuss the spectators were making in the right-center-field bleachers at the time.

He did a couple of woozy turns in the grass, the ball still lodged where he caught it, the crowd braying, and himself forgetting to jog back to the dugout because the side, after all, had been retired. Shortly he came to. "The bell!" he thought. "The bell!" And he began to move, to trot, to run, to run flat out, back to the pit next to the third-base line where his teammates congratulated him and he fell all over them, jabbering and joking, convivial as a Rotarian.

They thought he was crazy. Brock doesn't ever talk in the dugout! Listen to him now!

But *now* there has been a revelation, and a decision.

I am good enough. I can do it. I am staying. The bell just rang, and I am still good enough to stay.

By any objective standard there was nothing about the Pinson catch that warranted such a dramatic inner (for that matter outer) reaction in Brock. It was a splendid maneuver, but he had made some like it before, albeit not very consistently, and anyhow, it promised nothing in the way of sunnier days in the batter's box or on the bases, where he was counted on to contribute most. Nevertheless, that's how he saw it then and that's how he sees it still. It was the sword's edge of crisis, and once he had leaped it he was a major-leaguer for good and all.

In his own head, that is. That's where it counts, to be sure. But there remained a world outside that head too, where the likes of the Cubs lived, and the Cubs, remember, had other ideas about revelation. Furthermore, the rabbit of fear didn't die a sudden death, judging from the statistics columns. Brock continued to strike out, among a few other habits.

In other words the Brock destiny was still not shaped, nor his direction sure. One is inclined to think, after all, that any ballplayer who doesn't know when he has caught a line drive or hit a genuinely enormous home run still has quite a lot to learn about his own self-perceptions. It was true of Lou, God knows, all the way down to his last days with the Cubs and even, for a very little while, beyond.

We are now on State Street, great street, aorta of commercial Chicago, Emporium Gulch, where the folks from west of Halsted Street gather to spend the money which keeps the big beefy city's lifeblood clean—well, maybe not clean, but robust. A strikingly different breed from the Boul Mich-lakefront sophisticates, they are the working people who pay to see Chicago's professional teams play. So State Street now and then returns their mercantile favors by inviting the athletes to one of the big department stores, to give the folks there a little midday thrill. This time the place was Wieboldt's, and the shoppers got to see Lou Brock pick up his walking papers.

He was standing on a little makeshift stage, surrounded by a half-dozen other men associated with the Cubs, all of them talking fluent PR with the folks.

"Phone call for you, Lou," a voice said from offstage. First sportscaster Lou Boudreau went for it. Not for him. Then coach Lou Klein, Not for him either.

"For me?" said Lou Brock, and then to himself: "Only person I know in Chicago is Katie. Could anything be wrong with Louie or Wanda?"

It wasn't Katie. It was John Holland, the Cubs' general manager, who got to the point directly.

"Lou, we're calling a press conference for 1 P.M. You're involved. I thought I ought to let you know your contract has been transferred."

Lou froze, which I believe is what one says of a rabbit in a moment of acute fear. "Oh wow," he thought. "I almost wish it was Katie instead of him. Here I go: Tacoma. Here I go, and there go the majors. There goes the whole bundle." What he didn't have time to think but knew, all too ruefully, was that he was now hitting .251 in his third year in the big leagues. That's down seven points from last year, which was down five from the year before. The clock, I guess you'd have to say, had run out.

"We didn't really want to do this, Lou," Holland went on, "but the opportunity to pick up a front-line pitcher presented itself, and we couldn't turn it down."

Lou was trying to listen, but the airplane revving up for Tacoma was making a fearful noise.

"We are sending you to St. Louis."

That cut through it. "What? *St. Louis!!??*" Suddenly the noise resumed, only this time from a Missouri-bound carrier: heavenly sound, music to be resurrected by. He was, praise all the saints, still in the major leagues.

Today Lou is not sure whether Holland told him then and there that the deal consisted of three Cubs—himself plus pitchers Jack Spring and Paul Toth—in exchange for three Cardinals —moundsmen Ernie Broglio and Bobby Shantz, and out-fielder Doug Clemens. Brock couldn't hear much of anything, until Holland brought him around with the instructions to report within 72 hours to Houston, where the Cards would be playing the Astros. If he wished, he could leave as early as the 2 P.M. plane, just a little more than an hour from now.

He reassembled his thoughts and decided to depart immediately. He knew Katie was home. She had a day off from her job at the University of Chicago. Both the kids were with her—Wanda Lorraine, now two, and brand-new little Louie. If he took off this minute, he'd have time to see them all, pack a suitcase, say goodbye and beat it out to O'Hare Airport, in time for the Houston flight.

He returned to the podium and, on wings of song, called out to the audience, "Hey! I just been traded, everybody! I'm going to St. Louis!"

There was, he recalls, no visible reaction from the shoppers. After three years of distilled mediocrity, who was Lou Brock anyway?

4.
A New life
in St. Louis

It is easy to sympathize with Lou Brock's personal sense of relief at the news of the trade to St. Louis. Objectively speaking, however, he was hardly out of the woods yet; he was simply out of Chicago. There were just as many bramble patches growing along the Mississippi as along the shores of Lake Michigan, and he got the feel of them soon enough.

If ever there was a consensus that one club had exquisitely reamed another in a major player exchange, this was it. Cub fans hugged themselves with delight. Cardinal devotees sputtered and threw things.

"Thank you, thank you, oh, you lovely St. Louis Cardinals," crowed Bob Smith in the *Chicago Daily News*. "Nice doing business with you. Please call again anytime."

"Bing Devine!" one St. Louis writer fumed meanwhile at the Cardinal general manager—John Holland's counterpart in the deal—"You have reached the living end!"

In the eye of this hurricane was not Lou Brock but pitcher Ernie Broglio. Brock may have been the substance of what Chicago was giving away, but he was little more than expensive bait. Broglio was the big fish, to all appearances worth the sacrifice and a good deal more. He was one of the most respected pitchers in the majors, a standout curve-baller who had won 21 games for the Redbirds in 1960 while posting a classy 2.75 earned-run average. And just last year, 1963, he notched eighteen victories, with the help of a 2.99 E.R.A.

As of now, June 15, very nearly midway through the 1964 campaign, his season's record was admittedly below that standard. He had won three and lost five and had a 3.53 E.R.A. This he attributed to soreness in his throwing arm, but he claimed the problem was temporary, and the Cubs, hungering for him, had decided his diagnosis was accurate. At twenty-eight, Broglio appeared to have some very good years ahead of him, but above all he had already proved himself to be a topflight performer. He was talented and he was dependable.

And that was just what the Cubs calculated they needed. As of the time of the trade they had won 27 games in 1964 and lost as many; for them that was a more than passably good record. With promising young players like Santo and Williams getting better every day, and Banks still capable of power fully supplementary to theirs; moreover, with a trio of starting pitchers—Dick Ellsworth, Bob Buhl and Larry Jackson, who seemed to have come into focus that year—the Cubs were beginning to think the unthinkable. A pennant was not out of the question. The acquisition of Broglio augmented that starting staff to what one Chicago scrivener called "the best foursome in the league," and awakened recollections of 1945, the last Cub title year, when the purchase of Hank Borowy from the Yankees assured the Chicagoans of a flag.

Bobby Shantz couldn't hurt either. Though past his Philadelphia prime, the bantam thirty-eight-year-old had lately developed into a tough and reliable relief hurler. His inclusion in the package was like a little ribbon of gold around it.

As for the loss of Brock, well, when you get right down to it, *what* loss? The Cubs had been carrying him—the phrase stands—for going on three years. Here he was, for all that great speed and presumed promise as a hitter, with only ten stolen bases for the current season and a tubercular .251 batting average. If it was a problem of outfielders in the Cub future, it was either a small problem or none at all. There were several others on the roster—Nelson Mathews, Billy Cowans, Ellis Burton, and now Clemens—all of them with decided potential who could hardly do much less than Brock had done, and might eventually do a great deal more.

Meanwhile, in grumpy St. Louis: As for the Cardinals' side of things, they insisted of course that they had to do something to lift the club—21 and 28 at the time and mired in eighth place—out of doldrums that had been quite unexpected in view of the fact that they had come close to winning the pennant in 1963. They needed assistance in the outfield and they believed that they could attract it by drawing on surplus pitching talent (Curt Simmons, Bob Gibson and Ray Sadecki were left after the departure of Broglio). Lou Brock, added Bing Devine, is a player with more future than past, if you please.

It did not please. The St. Louis fans were no more consoled by that argument than the folks in Chicago were attentive to it.

I have to keep reminding myself that the subject here is Brock. It is not Broglio. Yet I can't resist dwelling upon Broglio. Even today he occasionally returns in the stilly night to haunt me. The reason is that I am from Chicago, and Broglio is a name engraved—*branded* might be more festeringly apt—in the minds of all Chicago baseball-watchers. We mean no offense to Ernie Broglio, a good and stalwart mother's son who was just as baffled and as monumentally disappointed by his eventual fate as the most religious Cub fan. But oh, what a demonstration of the folly of playing baseball on paper, that deal turned out to be! How smashing Broglio had looked, and what a flop, what an extravagant, technicolor failure he was in Chicago. He lasted a little more than a year with the Cubs before it became apparent the arm misery was only as "temporary" as the remainder of his pathetically aborted career. By mid-1965 he had disappeared, gone with the same wind that Chicago fans down through the years have seen so often whisk other worn-out super talent into town and then out again. Like Dixie Walker or Ralph Kiner or (goddam the Cardinals!) Dizzy Dean.

At the time Brock got to Houston to join his new teammates, he was not universally regarded as the answer to St. Louis' prayers, Bing Devine to the contrary notwithstanding. He arrived in the Cardinal clubhouse at the Astrodome shortly after game time on the evening of June 15, the same day he had been traded. He was savvy, or maybe just self-conscious, enough to know he would attract some kind of attention there, if only the way a new kid on the block does. But he wasn't sure what kind it would be.

His first sensation in the locker room the next day was that a distinctly different atmosphere prevailed there from what he was accustomed to in Chicago. For one thing, it was just plain noisier. Everybody—players, coaches, auxiliary personnel—seemed to be yapping at once, and now and then a particularly percussive remark would rise above the rest, followed usually by hoots and guffaws. For another, the place seemed messier, with equipment strewn around. It was a little like his sandlot days in Louisiana. It sure as hell didn't have what he was used to regarding as the dignity of the major leagues.

One voice now, loud, piping, audible over the din. It belonged to Curt Flood, the brilliant veteran outfielder, and it was addressed to everybody: "Hey, you guys, I hear that Bing Devine has been pulling off some Branch Rickey magic in the marketplace again. I also hear he has another deal lined up—gonna trade Bill White for two broken bats."

Much glee, and eyes riveted on the newcomer. The newcomer in turn, already more habituated than he needed to

During my first trip away from home I pose in my U.S.A. uniform as a member of our Pan American team. *James Washington photo.*

This had to be one of my very first professional stolen bases. It occurred in 1960 in the Arizona Instructional League before I ever played a "real" pro game.

I have just received the Northern League's Rookie of the Year award. It is 1961 and I'm 22 years old.

As a Chicago Cub in 1963 I cross the plate with what is, I believe, the first inside the park home run I ever hit.

enny Boyer and I collide in pursuit of Phil Linz's foul popup in the
964 World Series. On the next pitch he hit a home run. Oh well. . . .
orld Wide Photo.

Left, top) The catch of the Vada Pinson line drive in 1964 that went
.ch a long way to making me feel like I belonged in the major leagues—
 started a double play.

Left) This is an easy one, but look at baby face Pete Rose. He was a
.cond baseman then, and a fine one.

A birthday party in 1968. Orlando Cepeda and Phil Gagliano have ju[
given me a baseball cake.

Cepeda, myself and Hank Aaron relaxed before a game. *St. Louis Glob*[
Democrat photo.

This is a good example of the short hard slide that I favor. I'm safe against the San Francisco Giants' third baseman, Tito Fuentes. (1969) *St. Louis Globe-Democrat photo.*

Out against the Mets in 1969. I didn't think so.

be to thinking the worst of himself, tensed visibly. Then, unhabitually, he relaxed. Somehow the remark felt more like being hit by a cream pie than splashed with acid. Lou grinned and looked sheepish, which was the most natural thing to do and evidently the best, since the laughter that followed made it clear that Flood's little sally was meant to josh, not to bait. Nobody that evening presented him with a plateful of cookies and milk, but he felt oddly more at ease amidst all the horseplay around him than he could remember in the decorous but customarily solemn setting of the Chicago Cubs' locker room. He blinked, gratefully, and hitched up his pants.

And when Manager Johnny Keane called on him to pinch-hit in the fifth inning, he (what a natural sense for the right move!) struck out on three pitches.

Guess how he felt. Well, guess again. He had all the reasons in the world to feel like yellowing meat, but he didn't. As he trudged back to the dugout following his little ignominy at bat, he heard a fan yell, "Who in the hell traded for that guy?" and he glanced over at Bing Devine's box, where the general manager was slumped in his seat, wearing a face like a thundercloud.

In the dugout, however, there seemed to be nothing but the outdoor version of that same hang-loose temper that he had perceived in the clubhouse. He sniffed the air in vain for the scent of recrimination. The game ended and the Cards lost, and still no sign of the deadly, remorseful gloom such a situation seemed to call for. In Chicago the coaches would most likely have called the players to postgame attention ("to heel," Lou says), and ordered them to sit and think about the game in silence. "For fifteen minutes, maybe," he recalls. "And I remember I used to say to myself on those occasions, what the hell is there to think about? We lost, didn't we? Is there something more to think about? And the players would all just sit there and look around the room and then under their arms, like swans sleeping, and somebody might laugh a little out of embarrassment and the coaches'd say, 'Who's that laughing?!' It was like police court.

"But nothing of the kind happened in Houston that night.

The Cardinals came back into the dressing room and if anything, they were in a kidding mood. They knew they lost, but all they said was 'O.K., let's get 'em tomorrow.' And then, 'Welcome to the team, Brock.'

"Me? 'Welcome'? Well, maybe so . . . just maybe so. I don't understand it, but it feels good."

For the next 24 hours Lou Brock continued not understanding it and feeling just fine about it. That night, June 16, true to the irrational logic of the Cardinals, Keane started him in left field; moreover, getting the hang of the irrationality himself, he knocked out three hits, stole two bases and scored both runs in St. Louis's 2–1 victory. Hooray for nonsense. Didn't they used to call these guys the Gas House Gang? *Now* he was beginning to understand. And happily enough, the good feeling seemed to increase, not decrease, with the understanding.

The basic facts of the Brock-Broglio affair are now part of the lore of the game: One star rising as the other fell; dream goods. It is common knowledge too that at this point in the narrative Lou Brock was on the brink of the greatness that had not only eluded him till now but danced mockingly around him. It was 1964 the year of the chrysalis, the time the grub turned into a butterfly.

Patience, however. There is a prior question, which calls Brock's capacity for self-analysis into play. How come he went through so rapid a change? (How rapid was it? you ask. Well, it happened suddenly enough to establish him as a name player, with a smart, astonishing .315 average, and forty stolen bases, by the end of the regular 1964 season. Indeed, by the end of the World Series following that season—stats later—he was a star, a player everybody was talking about. Given the dim reputation he carried with him on that plane to Houston to join the Cardinals in June, such a transformation has to qualify as stunningly, perplexingly swift. It reminds you of faith-healing stories; and in a way, perhaps the association is not out of place.)

"Among the first things I noticed with St. Louis, starting

with those opening two nights in Houston, was that the club was run on the principle of individual independence. If you wanted to do something, you did it; you didn't have to fill out forms.

"You couldn't do everything, of course. You didn't spit in Johnny Keane's eye, for instance. Furthermore, there was a full system of signals from the coaches, as with any other ballclub. Nevertheless, if you felt like taking extra batting practice on a given day, you took it. In Chicago, somebody told you to take it. If *he* didn't, *you* didn't. Once—this was a major turning point in my experience, I recall—Johnny Keane said to me, 'Since you've got the speed for it, I guess you're going to want to try stealing bases.'

" 'Hell yes, sure,' I said.

" 'Well, you're on. Go when it seems right to go.' That's all he said.

"My impulse—my *conditioned* impulse, that is—was to ask him when that was supposed to be, Mr. Keane? Under what conditions? Who gives me the sign? Are there different instructions for right- and left-handed pitchers? But I restrained myself. It was clear he was telling me that that decision was essentially mine to make. Wow. I had to keep rubbing my eyes. . . .

"The Cardinals were a scrambling team. They were built for speed and daring. They played for one run at a time, not like the Cubs, who were geared for the big inning. Keane didn't tell me that. It was obvious. In Chicago it would have been spelled out, like in a grade-school primer. Even if the coaches there had said to me, 'Steal when you want to,' I don't think I would have done it. If you decide to bolt for second base, and when you're halfway there it suddenly seems a bad idea, you're not about to turn around and go back. On the other hand, the prospect of getting shot down and going back to the dugout to hear about it is not attractive either.

"So you spend your time at first base *thinking* about all this, which does nothing but give you ulcers, divert your attention from the action at home plate and use up precious time. The simplest solution is just not to make a run for it.

"Not so with the Cardinals. They figured if what you were good at was stealing bases, you may as well be the chief authority in charge of the question, when should that base be stolen?

"So you see the fundamental difference in outlook between Chicago and St. Louis. The two teams had more or less opposite psychologies. In St. Louis you were taught—no, you were encouraged, or maybe it's better to say they assumed it was up to you—to play from your strengths. In Chicago you were always being asked to concentrate on your failings in order to correct them. The strengths, supposedly, would take care of themselves.

"I won't say how it is with other players, although I have my own ideas about that. For myself, the constant labor to right my wrongs—with my strengths stuck up there on the shelf all the while, so to speak—had the effect of turning me into an overthink machine. I'm not sure I conquered any of my more glaring weaknesses, but I do know that I got unsteadier at the very things I could excel in. Little wonder they traded me. A .251 batting average inspired no more confidence in them than it did in me."

(This, by the way, is how Lou talks. It is from tapes, and not ghostwritten. Professor Brock at the dais, ladies and gentlemen, lecturing on Diamond Psychology 101, and making more than elementary sense.)

"In other words, Kennedy was right, that day with the signatures. The Cubs weren't dumb. Charlie Metro, one of the other coaches, used to say 'put your best foot forward,' which sounds just like what Johnny Keane said to me. But there was a difference between what was said in Chicago and the way it was applied there. You never knew how far forward you could put that foot before one of The Cops would stomp on it with his boot. All you knew was that he would. You'd seen it happen. Sometimes to your own foot.

"With the Cardinals, I knew—and I think I knew it the first night in Houston in the dugout after I struck out—that *you had a right to fail*. Failure at one thing was permissible in the interest of letting you succeed at another. None of this was ever really put into words, which was another nice thing about it. You had the opportunity to figure it out for yourself."

What Brock didn't say—and it's interesting that he didn't—was that he was finding a handle he had been searching for since he was a kid in Collinston. All the time he spoke these words I was thinking about the home he grew up in, where there was no one close father but rather a number of sympathetic yet slightly more distant and notably more mobile tribal brothers and uncles, as it were, who often came into his life abruptly and left it the same way. I thought about the kerosene lamps, the contemptuous white boys on the bus, and the lonely weekends back of his house, where he ran to escape the hotshot cars. At the same time I reflected on the pride of his mother, plus the pride he felt in himself when he was a little bitty scrapper. All of these experiences, it seemed, had hardened and maybe even generated his resolve to get out of Collinston some day—since Collinston was a better place for a shirttail tad than for an adult with a load of hay on his back—and to make it big somewhere else. To make it, above all, with dignity; what Momma had called Respectable.

The psychotherapy was now working, summer, 1964. Anxieties which must have been there in the first place if the Cubs' coaching staff had nourished them as vigorously, though unintentionally, as they had, were falling away like scales from his eyes. Contrarily, the determination which endured so long side-by-side, tiger-and-rabbit, with those fears, was at last dovetailing with the gobs of natural talent he possessed, to enable him to get the better of the fears. Suddenly he was developing into a hell of a ballplayer, but the change was mostly in his mind. That is where things were happening fastest.

There's scar tissue in Lou Brock, which is tougher than normal skin. It covers old wounds he prefers to leave un-contemplated, or at any rate undiscussed. That is why, I think, he doesn't extend his self-analysis so far as to dig deeply into his own psychic history. Nor does he welcome questions about it. Sociable Lou is steely private Lou. He sleeps peacefully, but with one eye open.

5.
A Pennant in 1964

It was a weird, wonderful, whooping, dizzy, agonizing and even tragic end to the baseball year 1964, the kind you want to remember so you can tell your grandchildren about it. Of course the Yankees won the American League flag; that may have been the only predictable thing about the whole business. Five pennants in a row now for the elegant New York beasts, who didn't even need Casey Stengel for this most recent of them. Yogi Berra was sufficient to the task.

But the Yankees didn't march in quite like the Roman legions. Berra in fact was on the managerial ropes in August, when his team went into a terrible backslide right after he had said publicly that they had the pennant wrapped up. As it was, they squeaked through on the next-to-last day of the season, breathing hard, with Baltimore and Chicago giving them fits up to the very end.

But this was a minor drama compared to the one that unfolded in the National League. If you think Chicago fans still rue 1964 for the loss of Lou Brock, you should talk to somebody from Philadelphia. The Phillies were sky-high nearly all that summer, and it was a foregone conclusion as late as mid-September that they would gain their first league championship since 1950. On the fifteenth of the month they were six games ahead of—well, the Cardinals, as a matter of fact, who may by then have been pleased to forget Ernie Broglio as they basked in the new glow Brock was giving off, but who were sufficiently disappointing as a pennant contender that they finally decided to fire Bing Devine late in the season.

Just about that time the Phils rolled their eyes heavenward, and swooned. They lost ten games in a row, and by September 29, with less than a week left to play, Cincinnati took over first place and the Phils never got it back.

Cincinnati was a story unto itself. The Reds' manager, Freddy Hutchinson, had fallen ill earlier in the season: cancer, as it turned out. There was something rather magnificent about the ferocity with which Hutchinson's team later came charging on under his replacement Dick Sisler; and something altogether heartbreaking about the way Hutch saw them die, as he was himself dying, on the final day. To enrich the irony, it was the Phillies who whipped them—clobbered them 10–0 in fact, in a display of almost preposterously futile power. Already wasted from his ordeal, Hutchinson hung around the game until the eighth inning. Then he made his way up to the Reds' office where he waited, hunched over in a chair, to greet his beaten young men. He never saw them play again.

The Reds had come close, but they skidded badly in their last series with the Pirates. Indeed, on the day before the season closed there was an outside chance that the race would end in a four-way tie. On Saturday, October 3, the Cardinals led Cincy by a half game, Philadelphia by one-and-a-half, and San Francisco by two. If the Cards had lost one of their final two games with the Mets, if the Phils had beaten the Reds on the following day (both teams were idle Saturday), and if the Giants had taken two from the Cubs, there would have been one great quadruple knot at the top of the standings.

It didn't quite work out that way, which is probably the only part of the story that hints of anticlimax. As it was, the Cardinals prevailed, and even then, they nearly had to mortgage the house to do it. Their last contest was with the lowly New York Mets, the expansion team Casey Stengel was now working for. Old Case and his boys made it a good show at least until the fifth inning. The Mets had lost all of 109 games by then, but just two days earlier they shut out the Cards on one run. They were perfectly cast as spoilers, and today, Sunday, they managed to act the role long enough to knock Curt Simmons out of the box and take a 3–2 lead going into the Redbird home fifth.

At that point the scales tipped finally and decisively. By the start of the ninth, the Cardinals had added nine runs to their first two, and it was all over except for one extra little fillip that is worth a note in passing.

Bob Gibson, ace of the St. Louis staff, had been summoned to relieve Simmons in the fifth: something of a desperation move, given the fact that Gibson was the logical starter of any World Series the Cardinals might yet earn their way into.

But the Mets rallied, and Gibson left to make way for old Barney Schultz.

Barney Schultz: Once again you must indulge me my masochistic Chicago memories here. Schultz had been with the Cubs until 1963, when the same bloody Cardinals who picked off Lou Brock a year later picked up Barney, in exchange for somebody named Leo Burke. It may be true that Schultz was gone to the minors by early 1964, but it is no less true that he was back in St. Louis in August, whereupon he proceeded to do as much as anybody on the team to clinch the pennant. Eleven saves he racked up, one of which came that last day, when he gently laid the Mets to rest.

Imagine then: a thirty-eight-year-old has-been named

Schultz teaming up with a twenty-five-year-old never-was named Brock—both gentlemen formerly of Chicago—to hoist the 1964 flag over St. Louis.

Coming off the field that day, Brock was in a near trance. Writers asked him questions in the clubhouse to which he managed only to mumble answers, sometimes making no sense at all. "That kid can hit," one of the scribes said to Dick Groat, "but I'm not sure he knows he's in the big leagues yet."

"Don't wake him up," said Groat. "Let him sleep."

I'm not suggesting that Schultz and Brock did it all by themselves. There were a few other players on the Cardinal roster who made something more than modest contributions. There was a .303 first baseman named Bill White—splendid athlete—and a .294 third baseman named Ken Boyer—copy that—who between them batted in 221 runs for the year. There was the no less sparkling Curt Flood, author of the remark Lou Brock blinked at on his first visit to the Cardinal clubhouse in June: a .311 hitter and a jewel of an outfielder. There were likewise a solid shortstop, Dick Groat, a brilliant-fielding second baseman, Julian Javier, a standout catcher, Tim McCarver.

And of course Bob Gibson, already grown into one of the best right-handed pitchers in the game, together with two colleagues of the St. Louis mound corps—young Ray Sadecki, sole twenty-game winner on the team, and Curt Simmons. Another of 1964's ironies, apropos Simmons: He was a castoff from the Phillies, who were, by the time Simmons had won sixteen games for St. Louis and was preparing to participate in the World Series, probably off somewhere opening their wrists.

It added up to a pretty good—call it a very good—ballclub, which was now about to collide with another. The Yankees were also gifted. Names alone are enough to substantiate that: Mickey Mantle, Roger Maris, Joe Pepitone, Elston Howard, Bobby Richardson, Whitey Ford, Mel Stottlemyre, Jim Bouton. But since the New York American League entry has had a bad time of it in the 1970s, it may not be out of place to remind young readers that talent was not the only, perhaps not even the central, factor in the growth of the unparalleled dynasty which the Yankees fashioned over the course of the previous three decades.

They just didn't know what it was to lose. So they never lost. Or to put it another way, so they always won. That is not so imbecilic as it sounds, and Lou Brock would by then have been ready to acknowledge that. He had had more than a few encounters himself with the psychology of winning and losing, and he was destined for many more. All of them would shape and finally secure an outlook which today lays distinctly greater stress on what an athlete knows in his head and believes in his heart than on what he is—merely—physically capable of.

b. World Series Brilliance

There is no finer distillate of a World Series rivalry than the one between St. Louis and New York. It has a tradition that has survived league expansion and the coast-to-coast musical chairs of today's big-time baseball. St. Louis may be physically closer to the Atlantic than to the Pacific, but when you think of the Cardinals squaring off against the Yankees, you conjure an archetypal American confrontation between big-city eastern aristocrat and scrambling western country upstart. It is natural for a good, hopping fight.

The Dodgers and Yankees have something going for them too when they get together, but it's not what it once was. Maybe you got my meaning when the two of them were in last year's

Series, 1963. For one thing imagine the Yankees losing four in a row, which they did. Furthermore, depending on the length of your memory, the Dodgers either looked like New York City immigrants, in which case the Series reverberated with echoes of something like a subway under Chavez Ravine, or else they stood for the unalloyed zap and glitter of California. As far as I'm concerned, California may be west, but it's not western country, and the new Dodgers don't have a history yet. Besides, LA runs on vinyl stardust, and if that's not quite your basic image of Manhattan, it comes closer to it than what lies out there in the flat muggy middle between the two of them. Igor Stravinsky or Andy Warhol could live on either coast. You'd never find them in St. Louis.

You'd find Pepper Martin, and I'll rest my case on that. The record book can take it from there. It says the Cardinals beat the Yankees in a classic Series in 1926, after Babe Ruth hit three home runs in the fourth game and old beautiful Grover Cleveland Alexander struck out young beautiful Tony Lazzeri—now *that* was high drama—in the seventh inning of the seventh game.

Two years later, the Yankees evened things up. There was another pair of series split between the teams during World War II, when there weren't as many stars around as in the late 1920s, but no lack of fireworks for all of that. The Redbirds and the Bombers always came at each other like two yardfuls of honey badgers.

And now they are lined up for the fifth time, on the opposite sides of beat-up old Busch Stadium—still and always Sportsmans Park to those of us who care—an antique arena built on what they used to call the Grand Avenue Grounds, where they were playing baseball back in the 1860s.

Well, what does it all look like to you now, Lou? How does it feel? Think back for a moment to John Holland's phone call, at Wieboldt's, on State Street, last June: "We're transferring your contract, Lou. . . ." Remember? How your stomach dropped into your shoe for about three-quarters of a second and then bounced right up into your throat as soon as you heard the man say St. Louis, *not* Tacoma. . . .

While you're recollecting sensations, how about the condition of your poor head that day you came to after collapsing from all your hysterical running around in the Louisiana sun? Can you recall how your nine-year-old hands felt after Miss Young whopped them every time you bobbled the softball at first base?

Remember being made a fool of by Muhammad Ali, you standing there with your idiot suitcases in your hands?

Being called a butcher by that Chicago writer?

Losing your scholarship at Southern?

Baling hay?

Not even knowing, for Christ's sake, how to flip your sunglasses out there in Wrigley Field?

Or hitting .140 your first year at . . .

The memories are tumbling too fast now, out of all order and sense for narrative. But that's quite the way they came to Brock in the middle of the night before the opening game of the 1964 World Series: all the bad scenes of the past, flying dizzily across a backdrop of present, magical satisfaction at having Really and At Last Arrived.

Well, yes and no. Brock was, as it turned out, very much a part of the Series. You can't argue much with his nine base hits or the .300 average they added up to. He was equal to his tasks, and there is no doubt Chicago and all the oafishness it stood for was behind him. Still, there is no point in denying that the best was yet to come—the best being powerfully good, compared with 1964—and that Lou would have to wait a few more years for it. Patiently, the way Momma taught him.

For one thing, he didn't steal a base. Not one, and the series went seven games. In fact, there were only five bases stolen between both clubs, which may remind you that despite Maury Wills' exceptional record of 1962, baseball players weren't running in those days quite the way they do now. Lou tells me the Wills example didn't really catch on until sometime in the late 1960s.

I want to go back to that Yankee aristocratic image for a moment. I've implied it had a little tarnish on it by gametime of Wednesday, October 7. I said the New Yorkers had had to huff and puff to win their pennant, and even then on the penultimate day of the season. I also mentioned in passing that the Dodgers, though maybe I should say Sandy Koufax, had pinned their ears back in the '63 series.

The dynasty was probably already grinding down; you can see that in retrospect, given the ages of people like Mantle and Ford. But only that way. The Yankees were unsentimental favorites 17–10 going into a series that opened on the Cards' turf. Whitey Ford was the starting New York pitcher, about whose prowess—especially in that crucial role—no more dithyrambs need be written. He had a 2.13 E.R.A. in 1964 going for him, which was a full run-and-a-half better than that of his opponent, Sadecki. I record all this because whatever else Lou Brock did or did not do in the series, he was classical Brock his first time up.

Classical young 1964 Brock, that is. I mean he came to the plate in the first inning, with one out, feeling maybe somewhat more apprehension facing the brilliant southpaw he was looking at than he might nowadays about a pitcher of comparable merit. But Ford made the adrenaline flow along with the sweat, and after fouling off five pitches, Lou lined a single to right for the Cardinals' first base hit. Then—it's like a recipe—raced from first to third on Dick Groat's safety and bounded home on Ken Boyer's fly ball. Two hits, one run, the game lead and the precious psychological advantage that went with it.

How many times have we seen that sort of fine husbanding of resources from Brock? If you are hooked on H-bombs like Ted Williams and Henry Aaron, you probably figure Boyer furnished the big clout in that flurry of activity. But Boyer, rightfully proud as he was, wouldn't have. Somebody ought to reckon some-time—I mean really reckon statistically—the occasions when

Lou has milked a single out of a tame ground ball or an extra
base running on somebody else's 98¢ hit behind him or a tag-up
run from third out of a short sacrifice fly.

Ask Ford. He tried himself, a couple of innings later, to score
from second on a solid single, and he got good and gunned down
at the plate by a perfect strike from the leftfielder, name of Brock.
If Lou didn't crowd everybody else on the Cardinal team off the
stage that day, it was because everybody else looked kind of
marvelous too, and the Yankees went down to their fifth straight
World Series defeat, 9–5.

Right fielder Mike Shannon it was who attracted the most
attention, with a single and a prodigious 420-foot home run that
hit a beer sign in center field, plus two R.B.I.s and three runs
scored. But the whole Cardinal outfield together drove in seven
of the team's nine runs, Brock himself getting two on a wicked
double late in the game.

And after it was over, Stan Musial, clad in unfamiliar civilian
clothes, reflected on the performance of Brock and his own
replacement, Shannon. Musial put the whole St. Louis season,
including the Broglio-Brock deal, into proper perspective by
remarking, "We never would have won the pennant if I hadn't
retired."

It was Bob Gibson's four-inning relief stint on the last day of the
season that led Johnny Keane to hold him until the second game
of the series. That now seemed an excellent wisdom. The
Cards had the momentum, the home field, their gorgeous
twenty-nine-year-old colossus on the mound and a warm feeling
growing in their innards.

The odds changed and the Yankees were down. They elected
to counter with a slender reed of a pitcher—in his youthful way no
less gorgeous than Gibbie—whose name, Stottlemyre, was
giving the folks around Busch Stadium somewhat the same
trouble ("Shuttlecock?" "Staffordshire?") he himself had given
American League batsmen during the few months he had worked
that season. Mel Stottlemyre, twenty-two years old and out of

Washington state, was nine and three, with a 2.13 E.R.A., which record he had rapidly assembled just since August. You can figure, in view of the strain on the Yankees at the finish, where they would have been without him. They knew; they promptly voted him a full Series share.

And didn't he respond. He and Gibbie were 1–1 at the end of five, though by that time, if you had been betting, it would have had to be on the big St. Louis smoke manufacturer. Gibson had struck out eight Yankees in his first four innings, and he looked for all the world like—well, like Bob Gibson. *You* think up a better simile.

Then, however: I'm not sure anyone advanced any good reason beyond fatigue to explain why Gibson came all apart in the second half of the contest. He just lost it, lost the fire, his control, the game. By 8–3, with Stottlemyre himself folding a bit in the eighth and ninth when the Cardinals put over a couple of meaningless runs. But until then the kid was pretty exquisite. We Brock-watchers would rather not dwell on this game overlong—or on the one that followed it, or even, please God, on the one that followed that, as you will see. It wasn't that Lou put on goats' horns or anything like that, it's just that immortality is not made of the stuff he contributed to the second, third and fourth games of the 1964 series. Once, against Stottlemyre, he shot a bad-tempered liner right back at the kid, who knocked it down with his bare hand and threw Lou out. All that accomplished was a few ulcerous moments for Yogi Berra until Mel recovered feeling in his hand. But Brock went for the collar.

And then he did it again, next time out, in New York. You'll find his name in the box score, with "4–0–0" after it, and that's all. He was just there, punched in in the morning, punched out in the afternoon.

There are days like that, when none of it belongs to you and all of it gets heaped on somebody else's plate. But you can't skip over this game just because Lou Brock might rather. There is the little matter of that one pitch in the Yankee ninth.

This was Mickey Mantle's twelfth World Series, a statistic which is one more measure of the grandeur of that old New York dynasty. It wasn't really his best either, all in all, and in this very game he had committed an error in the sixth that permitted a Cardinal run to score. No small run, moreover. Up until then and for three innings beyond there was some real mean double-dyed pitching going on in windy Yankee Stadium. The principals were the aging but infinitely gallant Simmons and the intense young (can you believe it now?—*intense? young?*) Jim Bouton, twenty-five, with his violent, straight overhand pitches.

The Yankees had their own run, which they had picked up earlier and nursed tenderly like an only child all the way into the Cardinal ninth, when St. Louis almost but not quite got something going and sacrificed Simmons to a pinch-hitter in the process.

So it's still 1–up and here comes the great Schultz out to the mound in the last of the ninth and here comes Mantle from the other direction. And somewhere in the grandstands there must have been some poor slob who at that very moment turned to a vendor and asked him for a cup of coffee—thereupon missing Barney Schultz's first and only pitch. If the man was lucky, he might have dropped the coffee all over himself and caught a glimpse of the ball Mantle hit disappearing into the bleachers. Th-th-that's all, folks.

Schultz, by the way, was beyond consoling in the locker room afterward. I guess if you're a knuckleball pitcher and your knuckleball doesn't break when you throw it up to Mickey Mantle in the last of the ninth in a tied-up Series game, and Mickey Mantle does violence to it, you just may be beyond consoling in the locker room afterward. Johnny Keane, who was not a knuckleballer, was asked if the pitch "did anything."

"Yes. Once Mantle got involved with it," said Keane.

The athletes' money gets divvied up after the first four games of a World Series, but in 1964 the fourth game was, as one writer put it, "so tense that the players didn't dare to take time out in the dugouts to make a rapid calculation of their Series swag."

Well, I don't know. Let's call that a figure of speech. Then

1964 was before the pocket calculator, but well after the first big fast buck of all time, and there must have been somebody in those dugouts with a pencil, paper and enough arithmetic to pass some kind of quantitative word along to his acquisitive brethren. This is a play-for-pay game, after all. Take away the second part of that equation and you get zero.

But it is a game too, which is what the writer meant to underscore, and the fourth chapter of the 1964 classic was a rouser and nail-biter all at once. Uneasy St. Louis had little choice but to go back to Sadecki. Ray hadn't been a worldbeater his first time out, but now it was either him or Gibson, whose weariness in game two had worn a hole through his talent—or Roger Craig, much too uncertain a quantity. The Yankees, riding high now and on their home grounds, could afford to rest Whitey Ford, who was feeling bad anyhow. They had Al Downing ready, a respectable pitcher most of the time and now and then a terrific one.

All the above is an accurate analysis, except that not an iota of it worked out. The Yankees fetched Sadecki a cuff in the chops, literally right off the bat, scoring three times in the first inning. Ray got the man out and was lucky to do that. It was Craig then, who came on to set New York down without a run for the next five innings. Then Carl Warwick singled for him in the Cardinal sixth and two of the next three batters also got on, loading the bases.

The one that didn't, by the way, was Lou Brock. Remember Lou Brock, agreeable Lou, 0-for-4 again today?

Anyhow: high tension, with Ken Boyer coming up. Talk about your money players: Boyer saw one of Downing's changeups strolling down the pipe and he pounded it out of the park, the ninth grand-slammer in Series history and enough, as it turned out, to even the Series.

The final score of 4–3 must explain why none of the players lollygagged around the rest of the game, and why that writer figured, however hyperbolically, that no one had taken the trouble to reckon his Series earnings.

But everybody knew what they were by gametime the next day, you can believe that, and it was the Cardinals who responded more hungrily. Once again they used the big blow to win—this time 5–2, on Tim McCarver's three-run blast in the tenth—and at the time it looked as if the home run was turning into the crucial tactical weapon of the series. Mickey Mantle had employed it in game three, Ken Boyer in game four and now in the last of the contests scheduled for Yankee Stadium, it was not just McCarver's effort that put an end to the affair, but Tom Tresh's two-run smash in the ninth which had tied it, escorting everyone into extra innings.

Tresh got his, by the way, off one Robert Gibson, and let's talk about that. For as soon as you mention Gibbie, you have to revise all the talk about the tactical home run. It was Gibson who proved the ultimate weapon in this series, even though as late as the start of this fifth game, you couldn't have begun to make a case for the notion. He had had a bad time of it in his only outing, game two, and if anything, he had more to prove now than to brag about.

How did he prove it? Let me count the ways. For one thing, he had all his stuff that day, and Gibson with all his stuff was just about as awesome a baseball thrower as God (remember Gibbie calling Him Big Daddy?) ever made. He struck out thirteen Yankees, most of them on a fastball that nearly drilled a hole through McCarver's mitt. (Tim handled it, by the way, a lot better than the Yankees did.) Gibson should have had a five-hit shutout, and no need of his batterymate's heroics in the tenth inning, but with no outs in the Yankee ninth, Mickey Mantle hit a tricky grounder which Dick Groat tried to take on the short hop but bobbled for an error. Gibson shrugged this off and proceeded to fan Elston Howard on a murderous fastball. Then Joe Pepitone shot a line drive that hit Gibson on the hip and caromed off toward the third-base line. Gibbie, reacting instantaneously, fetched the ball and fired it to Bill White, nicking Pepitone by a lash, at least in the view of umpire Al Smith.

Not, however, and to say the least, in the estimation of Yogi Berra and a small crowd of ruffled Bombers who protested the decision long enough—at least it makes a plausible hypothesis—for Gibson's whole side to get stiff and his arm cold and Tom Tresh to plunk his very next pitch into the right-field seats. The only thing you can say for that development is that it saved Stottlemyre from a defeat he didn't deserve.

In the field the Yankees of the series of '64 were almost unrecognizable as the inheritors of a great tradition. I mean they were unsure. The tenth inning of this game was a perfect example.

After White walked, Ken Boyer laid down a bunt (yes, Boyer bunted—first time that season). Pitcher Pete Mikkelsen for some reason froze to his spot. Pepitone at first started for the slow-rolling ball, but hesitated, apparently incredulous that Mikkelsen should remain so transfixed. Meanwhile, Bobby Richardson, who hit a ton in the series (.406) but looked palsied afield, neither charged the ball himself nor thought to cover first base and suddenly there were two happy Cardinals on the basepaths with about 67,000 disgruntled New Yorkers studying them sourly. Next man up, Dick Groat, tried to bunt White and Boyer ahead, but missed, thus leaving White standing like a Christmas tree between second and third. Whereupon Elston Howard resourcefully elected to throw to second, which enabled White to scamper to third and even to earn a cheap stolen base for his efforts. (That sound in the Cardinal dugout is the thus-far unlarcenous Lou Brock gnashing his teeth—very quietly.)

If all this so unnerved Mikkelsen that he worked up a 3–1 count on McCarver, which made him strain for a second strike by throwing up a fat pitch that Tim drove out of sight, well, you'd have to understand. Anyhow, that blow just about wrapped the game up, except for a typically quick and businesslike execution of the tenth-inning Yankees by headsman Gibson.

Oh yes, and for our own chronicling purposes: Lou Brock went into the game with a .118 average. He got two hits, drove in a run and came out at .182. I didn't say that soared. I'm just keeping you posted.

Lou's troubles were not as bad as the Yankees'. New York was down three games to two, and they spent their following day (time off for travel to St. Louis) as a lot of their fans spent it: brooding on their state in life. It wasn't just that they had fielded clumsily and run the basepaths poorly, but, worse still, that they had moped and fussed and nagged—in fact, just plain bitched—about it all to anyone who would listen, the press, mostly. So the press responded sympathetically by calling them crybabies, which only made them mope the more. They were not eager to go back to St. Louis. They didn't like it away from home. Busch Stadium was a dump. It had an infield that was too hard. And the umpiring had been lousy.

They were in a perfectly foul mood, just pissy enough in fact to rear back and beat the socks off the Cardinals in game six, right there on that old granite infield in front of those myopic umpires and everybody. Bouton was brilliant again, and so was his rival, Curt Simmons, though not quite good enough. Curt buckled in the sixth, when Roger Maris and Mantle hit back-to-back home runs to break a 1–1 tie, and the aging southpaw was gone by the end of the seventh. Barney Schultz came on after a short relief appearance by Ron Taylor, and Barney really took his lumps this time: none of Mantle's type of mercifully quick destruction, but a lot of tearing of tissue and bone—four earned runs in less than an inning. It was just bad weather for the Schultzes during that series. Even these days Barney would just as soon talk about something else. Brock might feel a trifle better about it. He got three hits, none of which changed things much, and he raised his series average to .269. Pepitone hit a grand-slam.

On the eve of the seventh and final contest of the 1964 World Series, the two most famous pitchers on both rosters were down with the miseries. The sore arm Whitey Ford had developed—which was partly responsible for his giving way to starter Al Downing in game five—was no better now, and Yogi Berra felt obliged to award the final Yankee mound assignment to Mel Stottlemyre. As for Gibson, he was a pillar of pain. His hip still hurt from the impact of Pepitone's line drive two days earlier. In the very game that had visited this woe upon him, he inflicted some more on himself. Once he was hit by a foul tip while batting, and on another occasion he took a bad fall rounding first base after having hit safely. He was a mess.

He was also, however, a big, strong, tough, mean man, and he started that seventh game; moreover, let me remind you, with 48 hours of rest. Gibson had once played for the Harlem Globe Trotters, and he knew what it was to live a really grueling day-in-day-out type of athletic existence. On the other hand, that wasn't the real reason he showed up to pitch that last game. As I said, he was just big, strong, tough and competitive. Magnificently competitive. Besides, Johnny Keane must have thought, who the hell else would I dare stick out there, with no tomorrow and all that money riding?

For three innings Gibson and the wonderful young Stottlemyre reenacted the close-quarters duel they had going in the early stages of game two. This time, however, it was the kid Yankee who finally ran out of gas, something he hadn't done all series long. Even so, the Yankees in the field deserved some of the blame for that. In the home fourth, with Cardinals on first and second, Pepitone tried to turn a McCarver grounder into a 3–6–1 double play, but shortstop Phil Linz pulled Stottlemyre off first base with a bad throw after the forceout. A few seconds later Mike Shannon singled, sending McCarver around to third. Then Shannon himself decided to try for two, and Elston Howard, caught flat-footed by the maneuver, threw too late to get him, while McCarver scored. So there was Mel, suddenly two runs the poorer, victim of the sort of cheeky baserunning for which the Cardinals were noted and the sort of defensive thoughtlessness for which the Yankees most emphatically were not.

But everything was stacked against the kid and his colleagues that day. He surrendered another run on Dal Maxvill's untainted single, and was gone to a pinch-hitter by the time the Cards next came up. Then it was Downing's turn to be abused. Brock, beginning at last to look like the jewel that had made the Cardinals shine late that year, drove a stupendous home run onto the roof of the famous old pavilion in right field. (If you can't steal one base, then earn four, huh, Lou?) Two more runs scored after

Hitting a home run in Japan during an All-Star foreign trip in 1968.

Contemplating before a game. *Spectra-Action, Lou Portnoy photo*.

Safe against the Cubs.

I didn't know I could jump this high. Neither did Johnny Bench. *Spectre Action, Lou Portnoy photo.*

hope I'm paying attention to what I should be doing here. *Spectra-Action, Lou Portnoy photo.*

coring against the Pirates. Art Williams is the ump on top of the play. *t. Louis Globe-Democrat photo.*

Bud Harrelson takes a late throw and Felix Milan backs up. And some fans support me with a funny banner.

The Florist. *Camera Associates.*

My daughter Wanda, and friend.

Lou Brock, Jr. challenging Pete Rose to a race. Chip off the old block.

I like to sign autographs for pretty girls.

(*Right*) I avoid Henry Aaron's late tag in a game against the Braves in 1973. *St. Louis Globe-Democrat photo.*

With my fiftieth stolen base in 1975 I broke two major league records: Most seasons fifty or more stolen bases and most consecutive seasons fifty or more—11 years in both cases. Our ground-crew manager looks happy, Rob Belloir looks happy, I look happy and umpire Nick Colosi looks bored.

(Left) I knew I was safe moments before on this play. But Denny Doyle, then of the Phillies, disagreed strongly. Ump Tom Gorman explained the whole thing. *St. Louis Globe-Democrat photos.*

Here I am sliding into Joe Morgan at second and being called out.

. . . My reaction shows how I feel. *Spectra-Action, Lou Portnoy photos.*

Rounding third. *Spectra-Action, Lou Portnoy photo.*

In the dugout between innings. *Spectra-Action, Lou Portnoy photo.*

A good shot of a feint toward third base. *Spectra-Action, Lou Portnoy photo.*

Looks like I'm swinging for the fences here. Sometimes that gets me in trouble. *Spectra-Action, Lou Portnoy photo.*

Staring down the third base line—and hoping a line drive isn't headed my way. *Spectra-Action, Lou Portnoy photo.*

Some loyal fans. *Spectra-Action, Lou Portnoy photo.*

Heading for first base. *Spectra-Action, Lou Portnoy photo.*

that, and Downing never did get anybody out. It was 6–0 going into the Yankee sixth, with Gibson apparently under full sail.

There is no point in prolonging this. Gibbie not only lost his shutout directly, when Mantle hit his eighteenth World Series home run, but went on to give up a total of five runs, all earned. The Cardinals meanwhile added a seventh. So game seven—St. Louis, 7, New York, 5—was neither a classic of suspense nor anybody's individual masterpiece.

On the other hand, the journalists were fully justified in crowing about Gibson and, while they were at it, about the whole Cardinal tradition. The big righthander had pitched 27 World Series innings, equivalent of three full games out of the seven, and when you add that to his contributions in the final days of the league campaign, you get a total of 39 innings labored in less than two weeks. Pretty good goods. In the process he set a series record of 31 strikeouts—better than one an inning.

Of course it was not just statistics: If you want, you can use the figures to make him look just sort of O.K. A 3.00 series E.R.A., after all, is not the stuff of legend. But Gibson himself was, standing out there on the mound late in the game, looking like a scarred sequoia, body all achin'. "I didn't think it was possible," said Elston Howard later, "that a man could stand out there and throw for nine innings after what he's been through." Johnny Keane allowed as how he planned on getting just six innings out of Gibbie, but the man wanted to go on, he said, and *I* say maybe Johnny might have been gutsy enough to lift him if he thought Gibson was too far gone, but I don't think I would have been.

And now a valedictory for the Cardinals of 1964. They won both pennant and Series the way they have won whatever they won in the historic past—getting hit all the time they were hitting, losing blood while drawing it, seldom doing their job easily, sometimes even doing it crudely, but never dully or by halves. None of them gave off the smell of aristocracy—not even Gibson, who was always more hero than lord. But consider this: Of the ten World Series St. Louis had participated in since 1926, they had now won seven. Of those ten series, five had gone the full seven-game route and the Redbirds took every one.

One conclusion is: Beat 'em in six or don't bother to show up the next day. Another, more realistic, is that of such history dynasties may not be made, but traditions most assuredly are, and the Cardinals had one of the richest. Hornsby and Alexander, Medwick and Martin, the Deans and the Coopers and Slaughter and Musial and Schoendienst—any one of the good ol' boys would have been proud to have the 1964 Cardinals as their houseguests. Gibson would have been given the honored place at dinner, no doubt.

But Lou Brock would have gotten one hell of a warm greeting, and maybe even a little more close and solicitous scrutiny, because he was younger, and the spirit of St. Louis expected him to be around a long and profitable time.

7.
Good Years— and 1967

In May of 1965 Lou Brock, playing regular left field for the world champion St. Louis Cardinals, was hitting .370. The prophets of St. Louis were feeling bullish. They had sat around all winter, caressing memories of the year before that made prospects of the year ahead seem handsome and exhilarating. They remembered that the Cardinals had the best team batting average in the majors in 1964—I forgot to tell you that, didn't I— and that their pitching staff, with a nucleus of Gibson and Sadecki, looked sufficiently young and strong to be equal to the task of keeping the pennant in St. Louis.

Does that reasoning sound fanciful now, in view of the horrors that later struck? I mean, the Cardinals finished the year in seventh place, with a won-lost percentage below .500. You figure somebody should have had at least an ounce of foresight to see that coming.

Maybe somebody should have, but if so, the indictment applies to more places than St. Louis. The 1960s were uncommonly full of teams that skyrocketed and others that plummeted clean out of sight. Look at the Yankees. They also concluded 1965 in the second division, and in the following year they took a lease on the basement—yes, I said the New York Yankees—for the first time since 1912.

Or *regardez* L.A., while you're at it—winners in 1963, they wheezed home in sixth place the following year, then bounced right back in 1965 and 1966 to win the whole bundle. Even the Cubs were entered in this Yo-Yo derby. In 1966 they became the first team in history to shoulder the Mets out of the cellar, but by the end of 1967 they had shot up to third place, their noses bleeding and their man Durocher graciously accepting manager-of-the-year honors. And who killed the Cubs' dream of a pennant two years later? The Mets, that's who. Is there anything left to believe in if the Washington Senators, recently moulted into something called the Minnesota Twins, can take the American League championship in 1965?

The answer is no, not very much. I never thought of it until now, but even conservative old baseball, like every other walk of public life in America of the 1960s, was an arena of shock and violent change. I will simply remind you—without dwelling on the consequences, because you can do that yourself—of Vietnam, the assassinations, the counterculture, the Pill, Pop Art and the rise of a new national religion known as pro football, which even had its own Italian pope named Lombardi. Within baseball itself, there was a new high commissioner for the first time in fifteen years: William Eckert, a.k.a. General Eckert, hired, so it was said, because the owners wanted someone in that post whom they could order around, so naturally they appointed a general. There was also the Houston Astrodome, a glass-roofed superstadium, home of the Astros *nee* Colt-.45s, later of Astroturf. For a while they thought of using colored baseballs there, which led some people in Texas to the conclusion that racial upheaval had gone too far. It hadn't; Mayor McKeldin of Baltimore, in what he must have regarded as a gesture of magnanimity, urged the taverns of his city to let Negroes in who wanted to watch the 1966 World Series on TV. August judges argued over whether the Braves belonged to Atlanta or to Milwaukee. Atlanta won this one well after everyone not a party to it was stupefied with boredom.

Now see the Athletics try to decide whether *they* should stay in Kansas City or go to Louisville. See them neatly resolve this by moving to Oakland. Look, look! See their owner, C.O. Finley, accused by his own players of planting informers in the team dressing room. . . . Judge Landis, he long daid . . . so Juan Marichal of the Giants takes a baseball bat to the head of John Roseboro of the Dodgers, right in the middle of a game, and gets off with a $1,750 fine and an eight-day suspension. And Sandy Koufax and Don Drysdale, also of the Dodgers (Los Angeles, I keep telling you, is not real), decide to negotiate their contract in tandem, become Siamese holdouts, as it were, and threaten to give up baseball for the movies. Enough? One more thing: Casey Stengel, getting out of his car on the way to his seventy-fifth birthday party, falls, breaks his hip and retires a month later, leaving the game for good. If that doesn't tell you what kind of jostling from fate baseball took in the 1960s, nothing will.

I got sidetracked, though now I remember why. I was saying that the Cardinals went to pieces in 1965. Just before that I said Lou Brock was hitting .370 in May.

Well, Lou went to pieces right about then too, which was a portent no doubt, but not what I'm getting at. For the Cardinals, 1965 was the Year of the Turkey, so having acknowledged that, let's ignore it and return to the personal fortunes of young Brock. And how he went to pieces.

Brock, it seems, had begun to learn at last that he and the home run were really not meant for each other. His 1964 batting average—.315 and best on the Redbirds—was composed of a wild lot of things, extra-base hits as well as singles, bunts as well as

117

sharp blows—and more than a few strikeouts. Brock was then as he is now a peculiarly changeable, if not unpredictable, character at the plate who would hit the ball into orbit one time, exquisitely weasel a pop single to the opposite field the next and then fan on three pitches in the dirt.

No one was harder on him than the great Koufax, who was, of course, hard on everybody. (You will recall, I'm sure, that this year, 1965, Sandy struck out 382 batters and pitched his fourth no-hitter, which was also a perfect game.) Sandy could turn Lou into a flopping marionette with his curve and late-breaking fastball, and Brock had only one slender counterstrategy. He was a pretty good bunter who happened to know that Sandy was a comparatively inept fielder of bunts. So one fine day in May Lou bunted twice on Koufax and twice got on base. Once there, of course, he was a major menace. Both times that day, he stole second.

So on his next trip to the plate he was hit in the back by one of Koufax's pitches. It is academic whether Sandy meant to do that; it was claimed he was above such low games, though Brock insists Sandy later admitted he was the only man the master ever threw at. The point is, Lou's shoulder blade was broken, and when he returned to action, his momentum was as well. His average fell to .220.

We are now at the edge of another of the crises in Brock's career, and the way he resolved it was not only characteristic of but central to his whole approach to the game. Moreover, we have encountered its likes before. And will again.

It was not the physical effects of the broken shoulder that caused this particular batting collapse; he was just suddenly scared to death of all inside pitches. So he kept retreating in the batter's box, while his average washed away. Finally one day, when he stepped back, it was for the purpose of giving himself a swift boot in the tail. He did not rely on any manager or coach to help him. That much, and it was no small thing, he had learned way back on a Louisiana grade-school softball field, and relearned in several more prepossessing locales thereafter. Dick Young of the New York *Daily News* once wrote: "He called a clubhouse

meeting. With himself. Just two people: Lou Brock talking to Lou
Brock, being tough with Lou Brock. . . .

" 'I made myself do it. I even closed my eyes and stepped
into a few. Then you hit a few and you realize you're over it.
You've beaten the fear.' "

Classical, concentrated psychology theory, of course, the
formulation of which no analyst ever improved upon. But as all
analysts know, it isn't the formulation that matters so much as the
resolve to act upon it. That is something Brock has become an
authentic master of. I am not speaking idly when I say some
university ought someday to do a formal study on him in this
respect.

Anyhow, once past this last hump, Brock had a better time of
it with Koufax. In fact he learned something more about fastball
pitchers at about the same time, by asking a question of one of the
best of the breed—Bob Gibson. Let Dick Young tell it again:

" 'Where do you like a hitter to stand in the box against you?'

" 'In the back of the box,' said Gibbie.

" 'Why?' Brock was surprised to hear a fastball pitcher say he
preferred the hitter standing away from him.

" 'Because the fastball does most of its moving in the strike
zone,' Gibson told him. 'You stand up front, you get it before it
moves.'

"Thereafter, says Brock, he moved to the front of the batter's
box against men like Tom Seaver.

"Thinking about the obvious, then being contrary, is the
secret of Lou Brock's immense success in baseball, particularly on
the basepaths, where he vibrates."

Back to 1965, and 1966 too, and good riddance to both of them,
likewise very short process:

Sadecki failed. Javier got hurt in '65 and had a terrible year in
'66. Simmons got older, just faded away. Boyer went nowhere,
except finally to the Mets for Al Jackson, who gave the Cards a
good year in '66, though to no ultimate avail, since LA won the
flag. Sadecki was traded to the Giants early in '66 for Orlando

Cepeda, another good player gone bad, or at least gone highly questionable on account of a 1965 injury and a consequent knee operation. (More on that trade later, accompanied by shouts of joy.) Flood did well in '65 (.310), unwell in '66 (.267). Then well again—.335—in '67, a fact that adds to what I suggested earlier—namely, that baseball in the second half of the sixties was consistent primarily in its mad inconsistency.

On the other hand, at least in St. Louis, there were Brock and Gibson. If the Cardinals languished, they pressed evenly on, waiting for their team to catch up with them. Brock recovered from his post-Koufax trauma well enough to post a .288 average for 1965. He got off to a bad start in 1966, going four-for-forty (striking out twice as often as he hit safely), and he even ended up on the bench for a time. But by then he was already accomplished in dealing with adversity. He would give it a lot of line when it struck, wait patiently upon it, then haul it in and clobber it on the head. Then he would go back to being good. By the end of 1966 he had more than talent; he had style, savvy and character. He settled down to being a player with weaknesses, oddly many of them the same ones he had suffered in Chicago: an inability to hit the curve, a tendency to strike out and to err occasionally in the field. But he lived with these blemishes and didn't kick himself around the block for them.

For he also recognized his talents—just as coolly and realistically—so they did nothing but grow. If he was an unpredictable hitter, he managed to exploit that very trait by turning himself into a crazily dangerous one. In the end, paradoxically, he *was* consistent. His 1966 average was .288, second on the team only to Cepeda's .301. And in both of those lean years for the Cardinals, he gradually and unceremoniously took over the league leadership in stolen bases. His total of 62 in 1965 was fully 32 behind that of Maury Wills. But Wills tailed off in 1966, while Lou came on strong with 74. By the beginning of the 1967 season, Lou Brock was a star, all set to explode into a superstar. Ashford Williams watched it all, back in Louisiana, his pride enriched, his faith redeemed.

8.
World Series
1967

Some years let you know about the passage of time more than others. In 1967 it seemed there was a constant changing of the guard somewhere, throughout baseball: old gallants passing, young ones coming of age. Whitey Ford retired. So did Koufax. Jimmy Foxx died. Can it be that late? . . . Neither Mickey Mantle nor Willie Mays was voted onto the All-Star teams of their respective leagues, and though they were later placed on the rosters in a gesture of veneration—what else to call it?—both men were called out on strikes in their sole appearances of the game.

Lou Brock, not quite twenty-eight, with a future considerably longer than his past, came face to face himself with mortality. His younger brother Curt died. Water pressure on the brain; it happened during the winter prior to the 1967 campaign.

"I could see him slipping away," Brock said. "And there was no way to stop it. He was twenty-five, man. Twenty-five years old. Gone for good."

Brock dedicated the 1967 season to the memory of Curtis, and in view of everything I know about him, I am obliged to conclude, however sentimental it sounds, that this commitment was no small factor in the stunning performance he turned in that summer. As I have said, Brock can be distressingly unimpressive when there is no incentive to move him. Conversely, he can do the sort of thing he did that year, starting with his first official time at bat and ending with a spectacular contribution to the Cardinals' World Series victory over the Boston Red Sox.

Opening Day, April: Marichal on the mound for San Francisco. He delivers, and Brock lines a single into right field. He delivers again and Brock steals second. Several innings later Lou hits a three-run homer. So it goes, down to the wire. He starts in left field for the National League in the All-Star game. He hits .299 for the year, an average which includes 21 home runs and a total of 65 extra-base hits. He leads the league in runs scored, 200, and stolen bases, 52. You got the tally sheet handy?—that makes 188 for the last three seasons. Maury Wills, now playing for Pittsburgh, manages 29 thefts in 1967. The King is Dead; Long Live the King. . . .

The Cardinals won the pennant in a walk, by ten-and-a-half games, wrapping things up three full days before the autumnal equinox. That is enough to tell you the National League race that year constituted no threat to sufferers from hypertension. It did cost Al Jackson a hangover and some financial confusion, however. After the Cardinals' party at Bookbinder's in Philadelphia, following the clinching of the pennant, somebody persuaded Al it was time for him to go back to the hotel. Peering through his champagne fog, he spied a cab, or what looked like one, and told the uniformed driver where he wanted to go. He got there quickly and gave the man a ten-dollar bill. The man wouldn't take it.

"What kind of crazy town is this, with free cab rides?" Al wondered the next day.

"That wasn't a cab, Al," replied Lou Brock.

"It sure must have been. Had a light on top."

"So do the Philadelphia police cars."

Now bear with me long enough that I can tidy up the place with a few swipes of the fact sheet; otherwise some names might get dropped which haven't found their way into the narrative yet, at least in this phase of it.

Johnny Keane—remember? Maybe you have forgotten by now, and if you have, you are forgiven, because Johnny, as it turned out, remained in the employ of the 1964 Cardinals little more than half a day after their World Series success against New York. Then suddenly he was wearing, of all things, a Yankee uniform, one, moreover, with "manager" written across it. Presto-change-o, just like that. Poor Yogi Berra meanwhile is standing there looking wounded, massaging his neck where the hook has bruised it. If St. Louis is all you care about, then the Keane story must end there, but I'm hoping you have enough irony in your soul to appreciate the fact that Berra went on to manage the Mets to a pennant in 1974, and Keane presided over that disastrous Yankee descent into the cellar of which we have already spoken. Ah fate!

Meanwhile, August Busch has built the homefolks a fancy new stadium along the riverfront, just a few yards away from another Titanic new object called the Gateway Arch, a 600-foot-high inverted U in stainless steel.

Meet me in St. Louis, it's a brand-new town. Bob Howsam has replaced Bing Devine. He has swept out several of the 1964 stars—Sadecki, Boyer, Groat and Bill White—replacing them with people named Cepeda, Jackson, Tolan. Now Howsam himself is gone to Cincinnati, and the Cardinals are being run by a couple of gentlemen not at all unfamiliar along the Mississippi except in their present roles: Stanley Musial, general manger, and Red Schoendienst, pilot on the field.

Musial has brought some young men up from the Cardinal farm system: Steve Carlton, Nelson Briles, Dick Hughes. Last winter he even picked up Roger Maris from the Yankees and persuaded the old slugger to give it one more try in new surroundings. Roger, beaten and torn as much from years of quarrels with the New York press as from injuries sustained on the field of play, acquiesced, and as it turned out, he and the Cardinals fell madly in love with each other.

"There ain't nothin' you can do for this old body," he had said to trainer Bob Bowman early in 1967, yet on one of his first outings in the new park, he stretched a single into a double by sliding head first on his belly, and after that the fans adored him and he adored the fans. "I know all about what Cepeda and Flood and Brock and Gibson and Javier did for the Cardinals in 1967," reflects Jerry Lovelace, the team's PR director, "but nobody will ever persuade me that anybody did more than Roger. He was a man reborn."

Now hear this: It is October 5 and the bunting is hung in Fenway Park. Bostonians normally give a damn about their Red Sox, but this season the affection was extravagant. The Sox had been something like a 100–1 shot in April. Two days before the end of the season they were one breathless game in arrears of the Twins, whom they proceeded to beat twice. All hell broke loose along the Charles. The atmosphere is electric now, which should, in view of all I have said, suggest to you that is the ideal time for Lou Brock to do his thing.

He did. Part of it, of course, was to do it before anyone knew he had in mind doing it. Before game one he was occupied as he always is shortly before a game, which to any casual observer consists in looking the very image of a man occupied with precisely nothing. He just sat in the dugout, chewed on a toothpick and relaxed. His eyes drifted over the field, stopping only now and then, and fitfully, evidently not studying anything much. In this case he was indeed thinking more than looking. He was reflecting on Jose Santiago, Boston's starting pitcher.

Santiago, Brock recalled, was the first Puerto Rican pitcher ever to start a World Series game.

So what do you suppose he's thinking about right now? Well, if I, Brock, were he, Santiago, I'd be thinking about being the first Puerto Rican pitcher ever to start a World Series game. A normal response, but a rather heavy load.

And what is Santiago *not* thinking about? Why, very likely not about Lou Brock, also normal.

That's all there was to the rumination behind the toothpick, but it sufficed. As Brock, first man to bat in the series, stepped up to the plate, he thought about Santiago thinking. Recognizing that that fact gave him a considerable psychological advantage over his opponent, Lou ripped the first pitch into right field for a single. Then, as the night follows the day, he bolted on the very next pitch, and suddenly the first Puerto Rican pitcher ever to start a World Series game found one of the fastest men in baseball on second base, in scoring position.

It doesn't matter much that Lou didn't score. I tell the story mostly to show what kind of cold-blooded fox he had grown into by late 1967. And after all, if this one maneuver hadn't fully succeeded, sooner or later another one like it would. And it did. In the seventh he got his third hit of the day and stole his second base. This time Curt Flood advanced him to third on a ground ball and Roger Maris scored him with the winning run on another. There was the recipe again: one run, one hit. Give Brock one base, it's as good as giving him two, or maybe even three, since he can score from second almost as easily as the average player can from third.

The Cardinals won, 2–1. Brock went four-for-four and scored both St. Louis runs. (The first had come in the third, though aided by the luxury of a Curt Flood double.) Santiago himself had homered for the sole Boston run.

"He was a very good man that day," says Brock courteously

and sincerely, not finding it necessary to add that only a psychological ruse by a man just as good could have tipped the scales against Santiago.

For game two, Red Sox manager Dick Williams decided to replace his rookie catcher Russ Gibson with veteran Elston Howard, formerly of the Yankees, now an elder statesman up Boston way. Did this move have anything to do with Brock's bedevilments on the basepaths? Williams wasn't saying, but Elston didn't mind imparting a candid thought or two. "When we played the Cards in the '64 Series," he allowed, "I don't remember Brock doing much. And when Maury Wills was stealing on everybody else, he didn't steal much on me in the World Series when we played the Dodgers in '63."

That's laying it on the line, Elston. No one can say you're mincing words. Now let's see if you know what you're about: Brock is evidently in a frisky mood this fall, and if you've a mind to challenge him, we ought to see some lively gymnastics around second base before the Series is over.

Rest assured we will, but before we get that far out on the playing field, let us pause at the pitcher's mound, where just about all the significant action of game two turned out to be confined.

Ladies and gentlemen, James Lonborg.

Twenty-four years old, winner of 22 games for Boston during the championship season, Lonborg was a former premed student at Stanford who not only read history books and listened to symphonic music, but did so, it was reported, voluntarily and unashamedly.

He is Boston's pitcher now in the second game, the early languors of which I prefer to dispense with in favor of the little scene enacted in the top of the eighth inning. With two out Lonborg, as he later put it, "hung a slider" to Julian Javier, who drove it into left field for a clean double. If Lonborg was an intellectual, he was no stoic. He threw up his arms in a gesture of exasperation mixed with despair. For good reason too: Javier had just gotten the first hit off him. By the time he did, the Red Sox were loafing comfortably, 5–0, and the only thing on anyone's mind (unless it was Carl Yastrzemski's two home runs) was Lonborg's no-hitter. Javier was not quite so happy about spoiling it as Lonborg was to have it spoiled, but he was in a grim postgame mood anyhow. He was a team man who had come out to win, not just to get his name in the papers. The series left Boston for St. Louis, all tied at one game apiece.

I neglected to say that Bob Gibson pitched for the Cardinals on the opening day of the series, allowing the Bosox six scattered hits and striking out ten men. So what else is new?

Come to think of it, Nelson Briles, and it is Gibson who furnishes the association. Last July 15, Roberto Clemente picked on one of Gibbie's pitches and drove it right back at the Cardinal ace. It fractured his leg. Gibson, true to form, pitched to several more men before the leg finally informed him it really was, like, broken, and not about to take any more orders from him.

Briles, another twenty-four-year-old scholar from the West Coast (linguistics; Santa Clara University), was in the bullpen at the time, and he came on to relieve Gibson. For all intents and purposes he never left. He took over Bob's spot in the starting rotation and went on to a distinguished season, posting a 14–5 record with an E.R.A. of 2.44, best on the club.

He started game three, working against Gary Bell.

It was Brock's turn to come alive again, after a futile day—like everyone else's—against Lonborg. Typically, Lou wasted no time. He tripled to lead off the home first, then scored on Flood's single. Before he had a chance to bat again, Mike Shannon had hit a two-run homer, but Brock returned to cause more trouble in the sixth, when he beat out a bunt.

I have only to remind you of the cat-and-mouse game between Lou and Wilbur Wood with which we began this whole story. Now it was Lee Stange on the mound, following the ritual of throwing over to first to keep Lou close to the bag, and finally throwing once too often. The ball got away from first baseman

George Scott and Brock flew all the way to third. It was then just a matter of Roger Maris singling him home: all very tidy, a model of economy.

That's classic Cardinal baseball and definitive Brock. I hope it is not lost on you that his kind of play, which is nettling, worrisome, exploitative and corrosive, can wreak as much havoc as the more muscular and overpowering variety. It is also considerably more beautiful to watch. The home run is a spectacle; a beat-out bunt followed by a stolen base, followed maybe by just enough of a hit to eke out a run—that comes a lot closer to art.

The Red Sox probably agreed, though by the end of game four they would have expressed their admiration for Lou Brock's style in somewhat saltier terms. At the outset of it they were down two games to one (the third contest had been settled 5–2 in Briles' favor). At the end of it they were even further behind.

It was basically a day of reprise: Gibson beat Santiago again, this time shutting the Sox out cold on five hits, while the Brock-Flood-Maris machine continued to raise its own special kind of hell.

The game, however, was never close. Brock beat out a roller in the first, advanced on Flood's single to left and scored ahead of Curt on Maris's double. Then—just so you understand what was meant by the new Maris—after Cepeda flied out, old Roger took a quick breath, tagged up and legged it to third, with the New York writers looking on, rubbing their eyes. By the end of the inning Santiago was gone and four runs were credited to the Cardinals. Two more came across in the third. Brock stole another base still later. Final score: St. Louis, 6; Boston, 0. Get out here, Lonborg, you're desperately needed. . . .

Jim did, in game five, and was splendid all over again, though there ought to be some word of praise for the six innings young Steve Carlton worked against him. Carlton gave the Sox only one run, and it was unearned. Yet the way Lonborg himself was cruising, it loomed increasingly large as the afternoon wore on. The Cardinals managed only two hits through eight innings, and when Boston put over a pair of runs in the top of the ninth, the

St. Louis fate was effectively sealed. Maris homered in the final Redbird stanza, but that was as much as Lonborg was willing to allow. He was a terrific pitcher that day, as he had been in the second game. Above all, he had done what he was supposed to do—namely, staunch the flow of Boston blood and get the series back to Fenway Park—where it might be not only evened up but prepared for the kind of ringing climax you could imagine if he and Gibson were to face each other. . . .

To look at both teams early that day of the sixth game, you'd never have believed the Cardinals were ahead of the Red Sox in the series, and in fact just a single victory away from taking all the bananas. The Redbirds' mood was as surly as the Boston weather. Like the Yankees of '64, they hadn't wanted to leave their home grounds for this last leg of the Series. They had hoped to conclude matters in five games, so that they could get down to the more serious business of squirrel hunting and winter banquet speeches. James Lonborg had mucked things up.

For Lonborg and his buddies, contrarily, life was a tarantelle. The Sox had finished ninth the year before, and they had gotten where they now were, late in 1967, by the grace of God, some spit, glue and a tire-patch kit. They recalled the recent end of the regular season, when in order to win the title they would have to beat Minnesota twice, and they had done just that. So they figured it was only, as one writer put it, Cinderellogical that they perform a similar feat in today's similar situation.

Allowing all of that however, it was still powerfully cheeky of them to assign the pitching chores to Gary Waslewski, a twenty-six-year-old rookie who could claim to be the least experienced starting pitcher in World Series history. Gary had begun eight major-league games in 1967 and finished none of them. He had logged a scant 42 innings of work and compiled a slender record of two wins, two losses.

On the other hand, the Cardinals themselves countered with a rookie pitcher, albeit a more worldly-wise one: twenty-nine-year-old Dick Hughes. You have to figure that managers Schoendienst and Williams were mindful somehow of the fact that the hitters on both teams were in a deep and apparently prolonged sleep. Only one of them—Lou Brock, with a .400 composite—was really sparkling, while the rest—well, not only was St. Louis batting .210 and Boston .206, but the total batting average of World Series teams for 1965, 1966 and 1967 was an asthmatic .212. So why not go now with a couple of greenies?

A little arithmetic from game six may furnish an answer to that. Hughes gained the dubious all-time World Series distinction of giving up three home runs in one inning—the fourth, which he never finished. Waslewski himself was gone by the end of six, plain tuckered out from all that unfamiliar labor. The Cardinals employed a total of eight pitchers, four of them shuffling back and forth in one inning. Two more series records. If the final score—Boston, 8; St. Louis, 4—does not indicate a slugfest of major proportions, it was nonetheless a day for the hitters to come roaring back from their statistical oblivion. Yastrzemski went three-for-four and Rico Petrocelli stroked two home runs. Reggie Smith got another. Brock himself propelled one of John Wyatt's seventh-inning pitches fully 450 feet up into the right-field bleachers, driving in the third and fourth Cardinal runs. In the third frame he had batted in the first Redbird tally, then scored the second himself, after stealing his fourth Series base. Oh, he was looking lovely all right, every inch Lou Brock, but the glow was lost in the sparks the Red Sox themselves sent flying that afternoon. The home folks could smell the approach of victory. It really had come down to the honey of an ending everyone had been thinking about since game five: Lonborg vs. Gibson in the last contest, second time in the history of the World Series that a pair of pitchers with two series wins—complete games at that—would square off against each other in the finale.

On the morning of the twelfth of October, Red Schoendienst decided not to hold a clubhouse meeting. "I had Gibson," he later said. "I just gave the ball to Gibson."

And Gibson gave it to the Red Sox. Uh-*huh*. Stuck it in their ear.

I wish more than you that I could spin a fine suspenseful tale for you now, about a clash of giants that was fought to the last, bitter, glorious, trembling corpuscle. But Lonborg didn't have it that day, and if *he* didn't, the Sox didn't. Simple as that, and no point in trying to make more of it. Boston's Cinderella story ended shortly after midnight on the metaphorical clock, when the pumpkins and mice took over Fenway Park for the winter and the Prince hopped a jet to St. Louis with one of the older sisters. The glass slipper? I can't resist recalling a photograph in the papers next day of Umpire Augie Donatelli. It showed him a few seconds after the game, gleefully—rather like a little mouse—running off the field, holding a couple of baseball caps which had fallen from their owners' heads during the Cardinal melee around the pitcher's mound. Augie no doubt was going to drive his pumpkin out to his little place in the woods, where he kept a trophy case over the fireplace.

Shortly before the beginning of the game, Cardinal bullpen coach Billy Muffett dropped by the St. Louis dugout and casually remarked to all assembled that he had been watching Lonborg during his warmups and the big righthander didn't look to Billy as if he had his usual stuff. That's the sort of story that may sound better in retrospect than it did at the time it happened. But retrospect is what we're dealing in here and, in fact, the top of the Redbird batting order confirmed Muffett's opinion after they had faced Lonborg in the first inning.

In the visitors' third Dal Maxvill tripled, Curt Flood singled him home, Roger Maris singled Flood to third and Flood scored on a wild pitch. Two runs for the Cards: Not only twice as many as they had scored off Lonborg in all their previous work against him, but, more importantly, probably enough fuel to keep big Gibbie running all day.

Just to be on the safe side, however, the Cardinal ace helped himself to a home run in the fifth inning. This evidently inspired his leftfielder to more of the Brockery he had already been spreading around. Lou singled to right.

Then he stole second.

Then he stole third.

And then he scored, after Maris's fly ball.

Later he hit a double. And stole one more base, which made a total of three for the game and seven for the series.

(Pepper Martin, by the way, during the 1931 Cardinal Series against Philadelphia in which he was said to have "run wild"—and in fact he did—stole five. Old Honus Wagner purloined six back in the Mesozoic era. Lou's mark was a record.)

I remember Lou telling me one day, don't get hung up on statistics. They are not a true measure of a player, he said, or at least not a sufficient one, and of course he is right. On the other hand, I feel obliged to say here that I got most of these facts from him. Mind you, it isn't that he is himself addicted to the heady wine of statistics, but that he has this weird and involuntary knack I mentioned earlier, for remembering numbers photographically. I recall his clicking off the story of the 1967 World Series as if he were reading it out of an almanac. It is an extraordinary trait. God, what an espionage agent he would have made.

Apropos personality patterns, let me remark once more here before we leave 1967 for blessed 1968. Lou often describes himself as "the third man in a two-man act." That's cute, but it's also damned self-effacing in view of his reputation, and your first inclination is to put up an argument against it. Your second is to wonder how such a proud man can say such an apparently unproud thing about himself.

But it isn't a matter of pride. He has enough of that, in fact, that he can afford to be realistic about himself. The realism, you eventually learn, is precisely what has made him into the kind of player he is, one who has spent his whole career making the very most of his gifts. He was nothing short of spectacular in the '67 series, and here I will defy his counsel by citing some more numbers, which I looked up myself: in addition to the seven stolen bases, a .414 batting average, a total of twelve hits (one shy of the series record) and eight runs scored (surpassed only by Gehrig and Ruth before him)—in short, a bunch of figures that easily add up to the most potent single offensive record of the whole 1967 event.

Yet it was Gibson who was voted the series' most valuable player, and Brock who concurs in the judgment. "Look what he did," says Lou. "He's a money pitcher. If you want one game and you want it worse than anything—in other words, if you want the last game of the World Series—you go to Gibbie before you go to anybody else. That's why he deserved that award."

As for the other big prize, the National League Most Valuable Player award for the whole season, that went to Orlando Cepeda, magnificently resurrected from his own personal hell of 1966. The Baby Bull from Puerto Rico batted .325, hit 25 home runs and drove in 111 runs. He was the big slugger among a troop of little sluggers on the Cardinals (they called themselves "El Birdos" during Cepeda's day), and that's the kind of muscle that builds the biggest headlines. Lou Brock knows that. He also respects it. "Cepeda earned what he got, every bit of it," he says.

Lou smiles as he recalls his old buddy. It is a warm and genuine smile. And behind the face that projects it is a cool, clear mind, utterly disabused of illusion.

Can you put up with a bit of anticlimax here, for the sake of lightness? It seems the boys at St. Louis radio-TV station KMOX felt that really, while Gibson's World Series was as terrific as the writers said it was, it wasn't so superior to Brock's that Bob should win a new Dodge Charger and Lou nothing more than a fond glance. So in a spasm of generosity KMOX decided to give Brock an automobile too. Lou's a good kid, right? And deserving. Let's ask him what kind he'd like. In fact, let's ask him right when he gets off the plane.

Lou figured the man with the microphone was just sort of flipped out over the pennant and the World Series win. People get like that a times like that. You can't really blame them for anything they say. So play along; it's all for laughs.

"I'll take a Caddy, thank you. Make it a nice big El Dorado. Best of the line."

Which is what came purring up to the curb in front of his house the next day, with papers and everything. *Hey, Gibbie, you getting good mileage out of your Dodge?* "With my big monster, I don't bother keeping track" . . .

With Tom Seaver. *Spectra-Action, Lou Portnoy photo.*

Safe against Atlanta. *Spectra-Action, Lou Portnoy photo.*

I thought I definitely had this one—against Morgan and Cincinnati. I am even more unhappy than in the previous Cincinnati picture. *Spectra-Action, Lou Portnoy photos.*

Here I dive back to second against Chris Speier on a pickoff attempt. *Spectra-Action, Lou Portnoy photo.*

(Left) I believe this was taken after my 105th stolen base in 1974. That was a wonderful feeling. *Spectra-Action, Lou Portnoy photo.*

I don't like to use the headlong slide, but this was an emergency. *Spectra-Action, Lou Portnoy photo.*

(*Left*) A beautiful shot by Lou Portnoy, a photographer friend of mine who has taken a lot of the pictures in this book. *Spectra-Action, Lou Portnoy photo.*

This is what it's all about. *Spectra-Action, Lou Portnoy photo.*

never gave enough thought to his outrageous remarks for you really to be outraged by them.

He played the organ. Said he: "The Series will be my biggest thrill, but I think I'll be more excited when I open in Las Vegas in two weeks." What can you say to something like that?

Gibson, who didn't play the organ, said nothing. At least not then. But when McLain announced on another occasion, "I want to humiliate the Cardinals," Gibbie remarked with dark simplicity, "If that's the way he feels about it, he'll get the chance."

The Gibson-McLain duality was reflected in the teams they worked for. As always with the Cardinals, they were scamperers who played in a big spacious stadium discouraging to home-run hitters. Lou Brock had stolen 62 bases that year, more than twice the total of the whole Tiger team. Detroit as a group, on the other hand, had hammered out 182 home runs in their smaller ballpark. The Redbirds had pitching, the Tigers, power.

Thus it was on October 2 that the two clubs collided for the first time since their one immortal earlier encounter of 1934, when two playing managers, Frankie Frisch and Mickey Cochrane, had led their charges all the way down to the decisive seventh game, which Dizzy Dean won in a romp, 11–0. If '68 was a plain jane of a year, the '68 Series promised to put some rouge on her cheeks, and, as things turned out, it lived up to the promise.

Seldom has a fall classic begun with more money riding on the two starting pitchers. And seldom did one proceed to outclass the other more decisively. McLain, whose excellent control was attested to by the fact that he walked only 63 men in all of 336 innings that year, threw eight straight pitches outside the strike zone in the third inning, and suddenly found himself with a pair of animated Cardinal runners on the bases behind him. Mike Shannon and Julian Javier followed with singles, in the midst of which Willie Horton committed a throwing error, and the Cards ed, 3–0. Two innings later Denny was lifted for a pinch-hitter, and two frames after that Lou Brock sent one of Joe Dobson's pitches 400 feet and out of the ballpark.

Gibson? He was a long mean scythe and the Tigers were a field of dry grass. In the top of the ninth inning, he peered down at Al Kaline from the vantage point of a five-hit shutout and struck him out summarily. He was not sure why this particular act was greeted by such exceptionally noisy cheers, but then he is too much of a businessman on the mound to give much thought to anything outside the perimeters of the playing field. Then he struck out Norman Cash. Same crowd response; same Gibson response to the response, though this time someone persuaded him to turn around and look at the scoreboard, which was now beside itself trying to inform him of the fact that he had just surpassed Sandy Koufax' World Series record of fifteen strikeouts in one game. Typically, Gibson returned promptly to matters of higher priority, which were dispatched with a final game-ending strikeout—the seventeenth—of Willie Horton.

"Well," said Tiger manager Mayo Smith after the game, seeking some measure of consolation, "at least we've seen the best now. It can't get any better than that."

The Cardinals' chief worry at the beginning of game two was the condition of Lou Brock's shoulder. In the midst of yesterday's festivities, in fact before Denny McLain had been given his quietus, Lou had stolen second base and mistreated his shoulder in the process. He hadn't given it much thought at the time, because Bill Freehan's throw was bounding out into right field, so Lou picked himself up and raced all the way to third. Once there, he became aware that he was not quite the man he had been a moment ago on first. Brock's attitude toward pain is essentially that of Gibson—namely, disdain—so he finished the game, adding that seventh-inning home run I mentioned, but the Cardinals fretted about him the rest of the day, and the night, and much of the next day, until it became apparent he was going to pay only a bit more attention to their worrying than he had to his own pain. He made ready for game two.

So, however, did Mickey Lolich.

And Mickey had the better of it, leastwise better than the Cardinals, whom he rather soundly beat, 8–1. But don't fault

Brock for that. He was just about the only live Redbird on the field. His associates managed only six hits off Lolich, a most unlikely-looking pitcher with a stomach bigger and spongier than McLain's, but an arm, that day anyhow, that seemed made of fine tungsten. The Cardinals got their sole run mostly on account of Lou's tireless gadflyisms. He walked in the sixth and stole second as Javier fanned. He moved to third on Flood's scratch hit and scored on a cheapie bloop single by Cepeda. The old Brock game: Invest a nickel, get back a dollar.

Trouble was, the Cardinals needed a sawbuck that day, and nearly everyone turned up broke. Lou got on base again in the eighth, via a single, but he died there. God knows he gave it the full measure, and even got Lolich pissed in the process. Mickey, it seems, thought he had found a way of coping with Brock. He let him take a fat lead, which Lou normally did not then and does not now do but may have, on that occasion, because the Detroit pitchers as a group were notorious for their inability to hold runners on base.

Lolich picked him off. Or rather, Lolich thought he picked him off. Brock, however, instead of hustling back to first, simply shot for second and beat Norm Cash's throw there. Lolich spat, then bore down and got the side out with no damage, but later he sulked to reporters that "Lou Brock is a glory-grabber."

Well, now, Mickey, there wasn't all that much glory to grab out there today, was there? Certainly Lou was feeling no better about the afternoon's activities than the rest of the Cardinals were, but he made no excuses for his style of play. "I'd rather hit a single than a homer when my team's as far behind as we were today," he said. "That way a pitcher's got to worry about me stealing and that takes his mind off the next batter. You maybe can start a rally that way."

But the St. Louis batters couldn't hack it in game two. Several observers, rather quickly forgetting the utter authority with which the Redbirds had won the previous day, remembered that the Cardinals had spent August and September in a state of relative lassitude, losing more games than they won. The word went around that they weren't sharp. That was nonsense, a product of the fickle atmosphere a Series generates. Later events

147

proved as much. But as the series moved over to Detroit, the odds shifted to the Tigers. . . .

It was the last time they would favor the Tigers, though don't make any rash inferences from that. Game three went to the Cardinals, 7–3, who won it by making use of the weapon that supposedly belonged to Detroit—the home run. In the top of the fifth, with the Tigers leading Ray Washburn, 2–1, Tim McCarver leaned into one of Earl Wilson's pitches and drove it out of sight, scoring two teammates ahead of him. The Bengals got one run back, but Cepeda put the game on ice with another three-run blast in the seventh.

That had to do something for the Bull's morale. Solid ballplayer that he fundamentally was, and superstar that he had been in 1967, he suffered along with a hundred other batters in '68, his average dropping to a woebegone .248. And what was even more acutely embarrassing to him, now, that is, was his overall World Series average, based on this and two previous appearances. It was .143. That is just not good for a man's health. A tonic was in order, and for most players there's no tonic like a four-base hit.

Unless you are Lou Brock.

If you are Lou Brock, there is a wide variety of ways of helping yourself to feel better, and Lou was in just the mood to call upon them. He certainly hadn't felt good when he went onto the field that day. It wasn't just the shoulder, it was the general indignities visited upon St. Louis in game two.

And don't forget Lolich's remark. Glory-grabber, huh? Lou, as I have said, is a realist, clear in his perception of the world around him and sure about his own motives, and really, folks, just about the last guy in the world who would seek his own satisfaction at the expense of the men he played alongside. Mickey must have realized that himself after his popoff. He phoned Lou later and apologized. "It took a real man to do that," Lou said.

Anyhow, all I have just related added up to the sort of

challenge to which Brock loves to respond, and respond he did. Leading off the game, he drew a base on balls and promptly stole second. Later he singled twice and stole again both times, so that by the end of five innings he had copped three bases. He got a third hit later on.

Now it was Tiger catcher Bill Freehan's turn to be unhappy with himself, or perhaps more accurately, to be perplexed about the whole problem of containing Brock—which was, after all, not his problem alone. "I can't throw the ball to second base until I get it from the pitcher's mound," he said after the game. And although Lou wasn't about to go too far in sharing his knowledge of the art of base-stealing with the public at large and the Detroit strategists in particular, he would have agreed with Freehan. It was not so much the catcher you steal on as the pitcher, he would have said, and the Detroit mound corps had not done all that much to protect the sanctity of the basepaths from marauders like Brock.

Freehan went on: "You can call for a pitchout all right, and I've done that. But if I do it too much, I'm only helping the hitter." His voice trailed off. Clearly the Tigers were worried more about Brock than about the two Cardinal home runs that had beaten them that day. After all, the Redbirds couldn't count on a regular display of that kind of power, but Brock, bruised shoulder and all, was a little like death and taxes.

He could, I might add, appear in just about as many different guises. Take next day for instance, game four, when he and Gibson put on a performance that quintessentially demonstrated why they were together the two best players to wear the St. Louis uniform during the post-Musial era.

Game four was billed, at least in some quarters, as the Big Rematch—Gibbie vs. McLain—although to take that seriously, it helped to be a Detroit diehard. More dispassionate souls were inclined to feel that after the first contest there was little point in staging another.

Indeed, perhaps there wasn't. Herewith Brock, entering

149

upon the scene even before Gibson: McLain threw him a strike to start the game. Then he threw again, but Lou connected and the ball came to rest somewhere in the right-center-field bleachers.

Thereafter, Brock got a booming triple, followed by a double, the last of these in turn by a theft of third base. He likewise batted in four runs. In short, if yesterday Lou was a capital vexation on the basepaths, today he was a rogue with the bat. Different emphasis, all right, but not the sort that made Freehan or the other Tigers any happier. It was the same man, number 20, doing it all, yet almost as if he punched a different set of buttons before every game he played. And for all the assortment of his approaches, Lou remained the most consistent player on the Cardinals. Look at the averages since 1964: .315, .288, .285, .299—and for 1968, .279. The last of these, remember, came during a year when hitters as a body were diving for cover. Brock's mark was only .005 under his ten-year lifetime average of .284.

Consistency? At the conclusion of the day's events, he was hitting .387 over a total of eighteen World Series games. And remember: We are not done with this series. Things get better.

For Detroit they couldn't have been much worse. What the hell was it with McLain? It's one thing—and bad enough at that—to hang one to Brock, but how do you explain the Great Humiliator a few minutes later dropping an easy throw at first base when he was supposed to be covering the bag? Call Smith Mayo the Merciful for removing Denny inside three innings. Maybe it was the fans, not Denny, he was being most merciful to. . . .

As for the Cardinals, they were in nothing remotely resembling a charitable mood. They scored ten runs on thirteen hits off six Detroit pitchers, while Gibson himself gave up only one run, a homer to Jim Northrop, on the way to scoring—get this—his seventh consecutive World Series complete-game victory. He struck out ten Tigers, making 27 for two games and 89 whiffs over the course of the 72 innings he had worked in three Series since 1964. He hit himself another homer too.

Oh, and one more thing about game four, just for the fun of

it. There was a one-hour-and-fourteen-minute rain delay during the third inning. When play resumed, the Tigers, down by four runs and not likely to get them back except by poisoning Gibson's drinking water, put on a monumental stall (in hopes the game would be wiped out before four-and-a-half innings were played), with batters endlessly retying shoelaces and experiencing abnormal difficulty in selecting bats. Meanwhile, the Cardinals, eager to have the game recorded, at one point instructed Julian Javier to "steal" second, and Julian took off well before the Detroit pitcher had even begun his delivery. Needless to say, the pitcher nailed him by a mile and needless to say, that's pretty much what he had in mind. Speed things along. The umpires saw it and decided to talk to both sides about their little childishness. Not good for the image of the national pastime, etc.

But that's all a footnote. The Cardinals were destined to win the game; there was no stopping them legally or otherwise. In fact, with a 3–1 series lead now, they looked like a sure thing to bring a big beautiful Tiger rug back home for Augie Busch's office.

Leonard Koppett, writing in the October 8 issue of the *New York Times*, remarked that Lou Brock was "the most brilliant Cardinal of this (or any) Series." Since the *Times* and its reporters are habituated to sobriety in the face of world spectacles, one is inclined to take Mr. Koppett's judgment with more than a grain of salt.

Casey Stengel, who never bothered quite so much with the judicious stance, nevertheless came to much the same conclusion about the St. Louis racer: "Nobody's been able to catch that guy. Not even the photographers with those long lenses. They look for him in the lens and he's gone." Then, ever the tactician, Casey added: "Tell me this. Why don't those pitchers throw over to first thirty or forty times? Maybe they don't pick him off, but they might make him mad."

There can be little argument with either view of Brock—Stengel's or Koppett's—given all we have said. Lou was skying, at an even higher altitude than the Cardinals as a whole, and both he and they picked up in game five precisely where they had left off in game four.

They did it against Mickey Lolich, too, the man who had tied them into such knots a few days earlier. But they were loose now, even insouciant about Lolich, and Brock showed the way his very first time at the plate when he whistled a double to right. Flood followed with a single that scored Lou and a few minutes later the revived Cepeda hit a home run. Suddenly the Cardinals owned a 3–0 lead, and Detroit hadn't even had a chance to bat. In the bars of St. Louis they started lining up the bottles.

And then a funny thing happened. The Cardinals lost the World Series.

It took a while; in retrospect—and especially if you are a Cardinal fan—a long and agonizing while. There are even some folks in St. Louis who, like the old Japanese soldiers lost in the Philippine hills, still don't believe it. But you can check the stats. The Tigers hoisted themselves up off the mat and won three games in a row, becoming the third team in major-league history to win a series after a 3–1 deficit. It was a marvelously dramatic denouement.

When did it start? What was the turning point? Most philosophers of the game agreed it was not the fourth inning when the Tigers got two of the three runs back. Nor could you regard as pivotal the steadiness that Lolich settled into after his near-disaster of a first inning: That was too extended in time.

The top of the fifth: That was it. Consensus. And wouldn't you know that it involved, centrally, Lou Brock.

Lou led off with another double, this one an opposite-field power shot that caromed off the wall. It was his third straight hit, and the pressbox buzzed with statistical comparisons, nearly all of which favored Lou. He was tied now with Eddie Collins for the all-time World Series stolen-base record, fourteen, which he had almost broken in the third, following his second hit. Bill Freehan had at least managed to throw him out on that occasion. Would he try again for number fifteen now?

Julian Javier got in the way of the answer by whipping a single into left field. It was a sharp hit, but Brock elected to try to score on it. He elected also, however, not to slide, but rather to beat Willie Horton's throw by running full tilt into Freehan guarding the plate. The umpire called him out. Said he hadn't touched the plate.

The play takes on a critical dimension after I tell you *a*) that Lolich didn't allow any more runs, and *b*) that Nelson Briles tired in the seventh when the Tigers scored three times to win the game, 5–3.

You see, there is one more thing about the 1968 Detroit team I haven't told you. They had a wicked reputation in the American League for coming from behind and winning late. That's what happened in this game, and as events unfolded during the following days, it's what happened in the Series.

Sensing this, or the imminence of it, the reporters were all over Lou Brock like a tent after the game. Why didn't he slide on Horton's throw? Had he really failed to touch the plate?

Brock answered patiently, once again sounding like a math teacher, quantifying his data, keeping things in their place.

"There were three sequences in my opinion," he said. "I touched the plate. The umpire called me out. The catcher tagged me later.

"Look," he went on. "If you run the bases as much as I do, you know when you touch the base. Many times I've gone into home with the catcher blocking the plate, but this is the first time I've ever been called out for not touching the plate."

Yeah, but why didn't you slide?

"The whole play was in front of me. I could see him and the plate and I knew what I had to do. If I slide, he moves both legs and seals off the plate completely. My only chance is to reach between his feet and touch the plate standing up."

I will leave it to you whether Brock was convincing. He certainly was analytical, true to his fashion, as you can read from his comments. And steadfast. He hasn't changed his mind to this day. If it was any consolation to him and his friends, he was hitting a mind-boggling .524 for the Series at the conclusion of game six. The to-slide-or-not-to-slide arguments piled up on both sides, along with a colorful little peripheral hassle over the way rock

singer Jose Feliciano had interpreted the "Star-Spangled
Banner" before the game that day. But in the end all the debates
were academic. The Tigers were grateful to be alive, as they
headed for game six in St. Louis. Some of them, in fact, were
more than grateful. They were even feeling a little hungry for
birdmeat.

The most sensational feature of game six was the ten-run
explosion Detroit detonated in the third inning. The last time that
many runs came clattering across the plate in a single frame was in
1929, when the Athletics rubbed out an 8–0 Chicago Cub lead. On
this present occasion the Tigers sent fifteen men to the plate.
Four of them walked, one got nicked with a pitch and seven got
base hits, the most destructive being Jim Northrop's grand-slam
homer.

But if that was the game's major spectacle, its real drama
rested with the redemption of Denny McLain. I cannot say how
chastened the mouthy young musician felt after the two floggings
Gibson administered him earlier, but there is no depriving him of
credit for a masterful comeback in which he limited the Cardinals
to nine hits and one lame ninth-inning run. He was fully on
his game. As for the Redbirds—well, McLain stopped Brock,
allowing Lou one hit (tantamount, under the circumstances, to
"stopping" him) and no stolen bases, and that is very nearly as
accurate a measurement of the overall St. Louis woe that day
as the 13–1 boxscore itself.

I am sure one's interpretation of the seventh game of the 1968
World Series will depend on his sympathies. If my heart
belonged to Detroit, I would no doubt see the Tigers'
resuscitation primarily as an achievement of doggedness and
fortitude. In fact I freely admit that Mickey Lolich, for one, had
every right to enjoy the silvery shafts of limelight that drifted
down upon him after this, his third victory of the series. "All my

life," he said afterward, "somebody had been a big star and Lolich was number two. I figured my day would come, and this was it."

Bloody right it was—for him and for the toughminded Tigers around him who, with all the ferocity of their namesakes, clawed their way up from the pit into which they found themselves cast by the end of the fourth game. On thirty separate occasions during the regular season they had won games in their last turn at bat. This Series triumph was not exactly new to them. But it was no less delicious and no less earned, for all of that.

But I am not a Tiger fan, and as I see that last game, my associations are with the Trojan war. When the goddess Athena intervened on the side of the Greeks, there was nothing the Trojans could do—no heroism, no strategy, no labor—to turn the tide in their own favor. Listen to these events of October 11, 1968:

Through six innings Bob Gibson had given up one hit, and even that was a scratch for which fate could take as much credit as Mickey Stanley. Dal Maxvill got his cleats caught in the outfield grass as he was trying to field Stanley's grounder, and the Tiger shortstop was safe. But he never scored. Gibson looked strong and sharp as ever.

In the bottom of the seventh he mowed down the first two men to face him. The next two singled. Then Jim Northrop, the frequency of whose name in those pages is a measure of his value to the '68 Tigers, hit a long drive to center. Had he pulled it, it might have been a home run, but straightaway, especially in the exact direction of Curt Flood, it was a pretty sure out. Flood was one of the most reliable centerfielders in baseball, a man who had once spent a whole season out in the garden without committing an error.

This time he slipped, for no exceptional reason, he later said—no banana peel or ankle twist or sudden vertigo. He just slipped in the outfield grass and the ball went over his head. It was scored as a triple. Two Detroit runs came home: twice as many as Gibson had surrendered in the whole series up until then.

THE BEST WORLD SERIES ANYBODY EVER HAD?

The next batter was Freehan, whose troubles at the plate that series were fully a match for the frustrations he had experienced trying to shoot down Lou Brock at second base. Freehan had one hit in 22 times at bat. One swing now and he had two for 23, the second being a double that drove in Northrop.

Don't tell me Athena hadn't bought a parcel of real estate in Detroit. Some minutes earlier the tireless Brock had opened the Cardinal sixth with a single. Remember, now, it was getting late and the game was scoreless, so Lou decided to engineer the same kind of steal that he had worked on Lolich in the second game. He took an uncommonly long lead, tempting a pickoff throw from Lolich, who bit at the bait, whirled and threw to first baseman Norm Cash, whereupon Brock broke for second.

This time the ruse didn't work. Cash's throw to Stanley was right on the button and Brock was out. And there's more. Javier followed this by lining out, but Flood got another single. So far I haven't said much about Flood's speed. I thought you might take it for granted. Suffice it to say it was comparable with Brock's. The three bases he stole during this series are evidence of that.

But in his haste (haste is not speed) he strayed a trifle too far from the bag, and the wily Lolich picked him off. For a brief moment he thought about trying for second, but a moment is an eon at a time like that, and he was destroyed somewhere between first and second.

There is more I could report here—a fourth Detroit run in the ninth, or Mike Shannon's homer in the same inning for the Cardinals, but neither of these affected the outcome. Nor would they help to describe the mood the Redbirds carried with them into the clubhouse after the game. All you can say is that as the years pass, the memory of each participant turns slowly from team delight if he won, or team misery if he lost, to personal pride for having been involved at all. And Lou Brock, with those seven stolen bases, thirteen hits, six extra-base hits, 25 total bases—all tying existent series records—not to mention a .464 batting mark, which averaged out to a career Series record of .391 (second highest in history)—had something to keep his recollections in later years warm indeed.

10.
Brock on Brock

It is time to pause and reflect, maybe to talk about some things we haven't talked about for a while. For instance, what Lou Brock looks like. I mean what he looks like now, in 1976; shortly you'll see why I want, at least for the moment, to leapfrog from 1968 up to the present.

He's handsome; I daresay that's the first thing you observe about him. It makes you wonder about his way with women. I can't really offer much authoritative detail about that, because I have been principally interested in him as a ballplayer and, no less importantly, because he regards his private life as nobody's domain but his own. However, I don't think I would be intruding rudely on it if I were to recall meeting him late one afternoon in a bar at the Hyatt House-Lincolnwood in Chicago, where he was conversing with two young women from the hotel's publicity department.

That, I must say, was something to behold. The two girls were in what is best described as a state of bedazzlement. No doubt this was due somewhat to the awe they felt in the presence of a famous man who was giving them his undivided attention, and likewise to the fact that he is a pretty gorgeous famous man at that, an athlete to boot. But what was unique to the situation was the way he chatted with them, the way he kidded around, and ingratiated, and clowned, and crooned, and bopped along and laughed that easy/hearty/melting laugh: the patter, the song-and-dance, The Line, the whole verbal come-on. He played the two of them like a harp. Including, as a finale, a mildly bawdy limerick that brought the house (of two) down.

So you say limericks are not your idea of sophisticated boy-girl conversation? O.K. Your privilege. But those girls in that bar squealed with delight at the recitation, and it was them he was talking to, not you, or me, or Red Schoendienst, or the patriarch of the Byzantine Church. Moreover, I'll bet he'd put the old patriarch at *his* ease too, though probably with some other kind of verbal gambit. Lou is good with words, comfortable with any and all he talks to, and capable of finding common conversational ground with any and all. I might just add that nothing came of that little scene in the bar. Lou smiled, rose, said goodbye to the girls and went on to some business elsewhere. It was all a moment in passing.

But that's tangential to what I was saying about his looks. He is not just handsome but a little on the timeless side. Now, at thirty-seven, he has begun to accommodate a white hair or two among the thicket of black ones ("I got integrated hair; those are my token whites"), but he is one hell of a youthful-looking thirty-seven. His body is trim and hard, without a trace of either fat pockets or the occasional telltale folds and sags of age which the average man cannot avoid even if he takes scrupulous care of himself. And I mention all this because I am getting around to the subject of Lou Brock in his thirties.

It is commonly understood that most players reach the peak of their powers sometime around the age of thirty, give or take a couple of years. Lou turned thirty in the summer of 1969. If the record shows anything about him, it is that he was at that time still short of the summit of his abilities. Check the stats for proof of this. After his .279 year in '68, his average rose to .298 the following season. Then he hit, consecutively, .304, .313, .311, .297, .304 and .309. Not bad for life in the gathering twilight. He has stolen more than fifty bases for eleven straight summers, during eight of which he led the league. There is not only no sign of decline in all these figures, but if anything, ample evidence of sustained and even increasing prowess.

How many players have come and gone—more to the point, how many brilliant ones have shot up like Roman candles and then been snuffed out—during the years Brock has maintained this really quite extraordinary constancy? There again is the paradox we have observed: Lou's baseball style is no style in the accepted sense. He can hit home runs, but he is not a slugger. On the other hand, how many leadoff men have driven in 76 runs, as he did in 1968? He has compiled a lifetime batting average of close to .300—over fifteen seasons—plus the best composite average of any player in World Series history—yet he is not renowned as a killer hitter. They claim, and he admits, that he has had his full share of fielding problems, but he has made many defensive plays that defy belief. Is he primarily a great baserunner? Careful with your answer: He entered the 1976 season leading *all* active National League players in total base hits, and has a lively shot at becoming the twelfth man in history to amass a career total of 3,000 hits. The only predictable thing about him, in short, is his unpredictability. That is his style; in that he is superbly consistent.

And bright, of course, though often in a most convoluted

way. I recall his response to the 1969 rule, which dictated lowering of the pitcher's mound.

"Other hitters may like that, but I'm not so sure," he said. "I know why it was done, all right. If you lower the mound, supposedly the pitcher has less of a height from which to come down on you at the plate. Trouble is, there is psychological height as well as physical height. The new rule only puts the pitcher more on his mettle. It is *his* own challenge to try harder, and you know how I feel about challenges. I'd rather they were mine than his."

Anyhow, this is all by way of launching a brief summary of the years that separate his two most distinguished feats: the 1968 World Series performance and the record-breaking base-stealing season of 1974.

The Cardinals faded in 1969, which would have been the Cubs' year except that the Mets decided late in the summer to commit their own first-magnitude miracle, which not only vaulted them from a ninth-place 1968 finish to a pennant, but even carried them past Baltimore in the Series.

The St. Louis story of the late sixties and early seventies was one of a team that looked alternately terrific and lackluster, but that never, in the last analysis, made off with the whole bundle. The glory and/or the lasting interest seemed confined more to subplots revolving around individuals. Joe Torre, who joined the club in 1969, played Godzilla for a few years, winning the MVP in 1971 with an average of .363 and assorted embellishments like 24 home runs, 230 hits and 137 R.B.I.s. In 1969 Gibson signed for $125,000, which, believe it or not, was a good deal of money in those days, in fact the most the Cardinals had ever paid one man for a year's labors. Gibbie responded rather the way you'd expect him to (you scratch my back, Mr. Busch, I'll scratch yours), by winning the National League's Cy Young award. One day that same summer Steve Carlton, so loaded with natural stuff it was fairly oozing out his pores, struck out nineteen men in a nine-inning game. Major-league record, of course, And then, Curt Flood and a whole new continent of subject matter.

The late sixties and early seventies were full of stories about a legal battle Flood set in motion which went all the way to the Supreme Court. He charged that baseball's reserve clause violated the national antitrust laws. He lost his case, and with it, for all intents and purposes, his career. While this was happening, a woman named Bernice Gera claimed she was being frustrated in her rightful efforts to become the first female umpire in organized baseball. She too went to court over this, and she won. After working one game in the minor leagues, as I understand it, she quit in bitterness over what she said were threats of physical abuse to her. Meantime, a couple of male umpires got into yet another legal hassle, with President Joe Cronin of the American League, over their own right to employment and the conditions that applied to it. There was even a full-scale strike by major-league umpires in 1970, and nothing less than a delay of the opening of the 1972 season, when the players themselves walked out in a quarrel with the owners over the question of retirement benefits.

Suddenly, or what seemed like suddenly, baseball—which we had for so long looked upon (how innocently!) as a game, an adventure, a sort of high bourgeois romance and nothing if not a relieving fantasy, with all the heroes and legends appertaining thereto—was in fact like the rest of our gray reality: a business, on which people's lives and livelihoods depended, in which such matters as social and personal rights and responsibilities of a sort we'd never troubled to think about were issues of substance.

It is hard enough keeping up with my own bank balance, not to mention the weekend batting averages. Now we find the sports pages filled with talk about lawyers and agents and player and management reps, expansion drafts, suits over new franchises and old ones, statements from congressmen, economic statistics and worse, economic terminology like debentures and cost curves and God knows what all. Forgive me; I just felt I had to say something about all this in the context of the early seventies and Lou Brock's early thirties. I don't want to go into it, because I'm not sure I care to understand it. I'd rather go back to the ballfield and the sunlight.

"Maybe *you* would," Brock said to me when I offered these

thoughts, "but some of the rest of us see it differently. I know the game looks very legalized now, but that makes it identical with God knows how many other walks of modern life.

"As a black I know well enough what prompted the civil rights movement in the early sixties. It was, and still is, an attempt to secure the rights of people who had been deprived of them. People who had their color in common. Other efforts have grown logically out of this; not just blacks looking for a fair shake, but Latinos and other ethnic groups.

"The way I see it, these early movements were aimed at social rights. But then they were followed by the women's thing, which was more an attempt to gain sexual rights. And what is happening now—the players' strikes are evidence of it—is an effort by people to get their personal and individual rights, not just social or sexual ones. It's all part of a series of revolutions in this half of the century, and they're not isolated. They're interconnected, and I think they make a good deal of sense. Just as it's harder now than it used to be to shove a black man off into the corner, or a Puerto Rican, or a woman—simply because they're black or Latin or female—it's harder to tell a ballplayer, an individual ballplayer: You are bound like an indentured servant to work for Club X until Club X decides to trade you to Club Y.

"Baseball is your entertainment, but it's my life, and in a country like this one, a man's life is supposed to be something important enough for the whole country to have concern over."

All right, class, any more questions?

It is 1973, and we have not only traveled a long way from Collinston, Louisiana, but put a fair distance between ourselves and the shaky days of Wrigley Field in the early 1960s. Lou Brock is a mature professional baseball player by now, a star. Is he a superstar maybe? Probably not. Say for a moment that he had decided in '73 to retire from baseball and tend to his floral shop in St. Louis or his Dodge agency in East St. Louis. It seems fairly safe to say we would remember him now as a topflight baserunner, all in all one of the best in the book, though a shade behind the great Wills, whose 1962 record he had never seriously threatened, and something more than a shade behind the still greater Cobb. We might add he was a pretty fair country hitter. Someone might take the trouble of looking past the record and listening to a few of his contemporaries tell what an elegant pressure player he could be, and what an unpleasant prospect it was for a pitcher to have to face him because while he wouldn't necessarily break a game wide open, not being Aaron and all—though he could do that too—he had the wicked knack of starting rallies, of turning a game around and just generally worrying you to death because you didn't know what he was going to do next.

But that is the mark of stars, as I said, not superstars, just so we understand each other. Lou understood, recognizing that he hadn't been with a pennant winner for a while, and that sometimes deprives a man of at least a little of the light that reflected, say, on some of the great Yankees of the fifties and early sixties and helped them glow like legends. Other times he would think, why can't a stolen base be reckoned as part of your total-base record? After all, if you hit a double, it goes into the book as two bases, so why couldn't a single followed by a steal be figured the same way? If it were, my record might look, you know, more formidable. . . .

But at about that point in his thinking the old realism would intercede, and he would say to himself, cut out the dreaming and the self-indulgence and get back to what you do best and what you know about yourself. Ever since the day you first joined the Cardinals in Houston, when you struck out nobody in the dugout groused at you for it, or said—as they did endlessly in Chicago—go out and CORRECT THAT WEAKNESS, you have made a point of playing from your strengths, of adapting what you do best to any given situation and not mooning over the things you couldn't do. Hell, you can't pitch like Gibson, and he likes to remind you you can't dance worth pocket lint . . . will you worry over that? . . . He can't hit like you, either, and he's no Nureyev himself, come to think of it. Do what you can do. Don't fret that you're not carved on the side of Mt. Rushmore.

At least not yet. . . .

Did I say it was 1973? It was in fact the late summer of 1973, about which time the Cardinals were beginning to look like serious pennant contenders again. Lou and the St. Louis managing staff decided one day that there might be something more he could do to help.

It was one of those decisions that was based less on any new knowledge than on the conscious and deliberate exploitation of what was already known. Everybody was aware that Lou was fast, that he was a good hitter who got on base a lot. Therefore, colleagues, let us here and now act upon the intelligence that the stolen base is more than a gesture to upset the opposition's pitcher, more than a momentary game-enhancing thrill. It is a decisive and major offensive weapon. Yes, this is common knowledge, but maybe that's the trouble with it: It is so common we haven't taken advantage of it. Get Lou on first base and he's as good as on second, which means as good as home on any kind of subsequent decent single, and some indecent ones. Get him on third with less than two out and he's in on a fly. To be sure, a home run is a simpler strategem, but things have never been simple for the Cardinals.

They were especially tough in '73—not only for St. Louis but for the several other teams with whom St. Louis was most closely competing. In 1969 the National League—like the American—expanded to include so many clubs, twelve, that two separate groupings of six were set up. The Redbirds had been assigned to the Eastern Division, all of whose member aggregations fell far short of splendor in 1973. The Cards wound up in second place, missing the division title by a scant one-and-a-half games, yet losing as many contests over the season—81—as they won. (San Francisco finished eleven games out in the West, with a record that would have beaten the Eastern champion Mets by five-and-a-half games.)

To this may be added some rather bleak Cardinal team statistics. Only young Ted Simmons hit for power, and he alone managed to hike his average up over .300. The rest of the St.

Louis batting order was barely O.K. Ditto the pitching, which featured only one starter with an E.R.A. under 3.00 (Gibson, who won only twelve games).

In short, the Cardinals had to heave and sweat for everything they got, and as the summer wore on, Lou Brock's potential on the basepaths became more and more a strategic, not merely a tactical, weapon. He stole over thirty bases in his last thirty games. Since the Cardinals lost the pennant, this was not a fact of earth-shaking relevance. But it had a lot to do with the way he conducted himself in 1974.

"I suspect every one of us judges the guys we play against by mixing up the picture we have of ourselves with the pictures we have of them. That's another way of saying we don't always see with objectivity. But we observe things the fans don't, or the writers, so I don't worry too much about the fairness of it all.

"Sure, I have strong opinions about the best pitchers I ever saw. You just gotta remember those opinions are formed mostly in the batter's box. There you can watch a man from a closer vantage point than any spectators in the stands have—especially the ones with the typewriters, who are oftentimes surer than they have any right to be that a particular pitch was a slider or a screwball. On the other hand, when you're in the box you're so busy concentrating on what you're doing that some aspects of the men you're facing may escape you. It reminds me of the blind men trying to describe the elephant.

"Suppose you ask me to list the greatest pitchers of my own time, and I start by saying Koufax, and Drysdale, and Marichal, and maybe Jim Maloney . . . and Bob Veale . . . and you say, 'Bob Veale? How do you figure Bob Veale belongs with all those other great ones?' Well, if you're so sure the others were great ones and Veale wasn't, why are you asking *me* in the first place? Maybe I got a cockeyed view of Veale, but he looked awfully good to me, and it's these eyes gotta do the judging.

"I'm tempted to go to the record book and show you where it

165

says he had a lifetime E.R.A. of just a hair over three, which is better than some of the so-called immortals posted. But that would be a rationalization.

"The fact is, he just gave me fits. First of all, he was a lefthander, and lefthanders as a class do not fill my heart with delight. Second, he could blow the ball past me like I was a birthday candle. I think he threw about as hard as anyone I ever faced in the major leagues. It's true he was a little bit wild sometimes. And very wild others. And he didn't have the best eyes. I mean he wore glasses that looked like the bottom of Coke bottles.

"On a real hot day out there, Veale would lather up a pretty fine sweat. He used to wear a bandanna to catch the moisture, much like the kind Rick Wise wears, I seem to recall.

"But it didn't always do much good. Inevitably those glasses would get all fogged up, and that could be as irritating to Veale as it was a danger to the life of anyone he was pitching to.

"One night I guess he'd had it with the cheaters, and he took 'em off and smashed 'em to bits. Right out there on the pitcher's mound. Scattered the pieces all over the ground. So I stepped out of the batter's box, naturally, 'cause Veale even when he could see, had trouble finding the plate with his pitches. More likely he'd find you, and like I said, he threw hard.

"So he says to the umpire, 'I'm ready.' And the ump says, 'O.K. Play ball!'

" 'Not me,' I said. 'I'm not going against that man until they go back to the clubhouse and get him another pair of glasses.' And I didn't budge.

"Well, they got him the glasses. Must have taken twenty minutes. And he proceeded to strike me out on three pitches. Very fast ones. I couldn't see them any better than he could.

"Back in the clubhouse later, somebody said to me, 'You took up all that time just so Veale could do *that* to you?'

" 'Well,' I said, 'at least I made it back to the dugout. I even had an outside chance with him. If his glasses had been off, more 'n likely I'd have nothing but a very sore body, or maybe no head left.' Remember to put down that later in the same game Veale creamed me with a pitch, and I wound up in the hospital.

"But Veale was not the hardest thrower I ever saw, come to think of it. Or the one with the least control, for that matter. There was a pitcher I played against in the Instructional League who threw smoke that was just awesome. He likewise had to be the wildest guy who ever put on a baseball uniform. He was Steve Dalkowsky; worked with the Baltimore organization. They built a wooden chute for him to throw at out in Arizona so he could practice hitting a target. He hit it all right. He broke the damn thing into splinters the first time he threw at it. There was lumber in it three-quarters-of-an-inch thick.

"He never succeeded in the majors, mostly because of his wildness, but he sure gave me some memorable moments before he hung it all up. He had eyes like Veale's, by the way. Same kind of glasses that looked thick enough to stop machine-gun bullets. Once I saw him throw a pitch that sailed clear over the head of the man in the on-deck circle. You hear stories like that about Ryne Duren, but I can't believe Ryne had anything on Dalkowski. When Steve took the mound, everybody in both dugouts put their batting helmets on.

"First time I ever watched him pitch, I was playing against him, and I led off the game. Being a rookie, I knew I had to stand my ground, so I tried to be just as aggressive as he was. On the first pitch I lifted my right foot to swing at the ball. I never even got the foot back on the ground before his throw had turned my helmet 180° around on my head. By the way, someone told me later that he had a sore arm at the time.

"Naturally you think highly of pitchers who were hard on you. I think I have a pretty good eye for those I've done well against too. Juan Marichal was just about as good a craftsman on the mound as I ever played against. He was exactly that—a master of his art. He paid very careful attention to every detail of the game, and I have a lot of respect for anybody like that. He was a pretty nifty psychologist too.

"One day I met him in the airport and he comes up to me and

says, 'Ah, Lou Brock. You are good hitter. You always hit very well against me.'

" 'Naw, I don't really,' I said, knowing full well I damn near owned him. 'Yes,' he said, 'I keep record. You hit me better than .350, you know that?'

"Well, it might have been a little better than that, I thought to myself. Don't undersell me, Marichal. But I still sort of marveled at this terrific pitcher coming on so modest with me. And I fell for it. I said, 'No, Juan, I always have trouble with you. You got a damn good screwball, you know that?' Sweet talk for sweet talk, I thought . . . tit for tat. Well, don't you know he started giving me nothing but screwballs after that day, and my average against him dropped almost out of sight for a while. He'd tricked me, same way I like to trick other guys. I learned something from that. Don't ever tell a pitcher anything.

"Don't ask him for favors either. One time I did that with Tom Seaver, and I've been paying for it ever since. It was like this:

"I started my first All-Star game in 1967. It was a big moment for me, because it was the first year Willie Mays hadn't started for the National League in over a decade, and I was out there in his place. So I was pretty excited about the prospect, and I got out to the clubhouse early that day. Before anyone else. And there were the clubhouse assistants buzzing around, as they always do . . . young kids, you know, about sixteen or seventeen, and I said to one of the youngest-looking of them, 'Hey, get me a Coke, will you?'

"Well, he hesitated for a moment, but then he went and got the Coke and came back and said, 'You're Lou Brock, aren't you? Pleased to meet you. I'm Tom Seaver.'

"Two inches tall is how I felt. He laughed and eased me out of that one. We had a good time together, and I've had plenty of admiration for him ever since. If anything, more than I wish I had. He charged me a dear price for that Coke. There was once a time when I hit him pretty good, but he's been rough to handle last couple of years. Strikes me out twice a game now, seems like.

"That All-Star game was in Anaheim, and I got a touch of Hollywood show biz on the occasion. Joey Bishop invited me to his talk show the night before the game, and Buddy Hackett and Joey and I spent some time on the subject of baseball superstitions. Hackett said, 'You don't believe in that stuff, do you, Lou?'

" 'Oh yes I do,' I said. 'I make a point never to walk on the foul line and never to step on a base when I'm going out to my position or coming in from it.'

" 'Why that's for the birds,' said Buddy, and he got me to agree to test my—what'll I call it, my theory—by stepping on second base when I went out on the field at the start of the game.

"I did, and the first batter—Tony Oliva—drove me back to the wall on a fly ball I just barely caught. Next night I was on the Bishop show again and so was Buddy. He said, 'Well, that proves I was right, doesn't it?'

"Not exactly,' I said. 'Check the film clips.' We did, and they showed me just nicking the edge of second with my shoe as I was taking the field. 'Now suppose I had stepped directly on that base, Buddy,' I said. 'You know perfectly well Oliva's drive wouldn't have come down yet. You won't ever catch me near that bag again.'

"I'll even go so far as to suggest that Al Hrabosky has arrived at that crazy little act of his by the superstition route, at least to some extent. Hell, I know it's all in the mind, but you'll do anything to win, including wearing the same underwear, like they say, for the duration of a batting streak. That would be enough by itself to frighten off the opposition, wouldn't it? Anyhow, I imagine one day Al found out by accident that by strolling out behind the mound between pitches and going through that zany pout of his—we really prefer to call it meditation—he could get the opposing batter unnerved. So he's been doing it ever since, like me avoiding that bag, 'cause it seems to work. I do admit it helps to be a gutty, aggressive type like Al. If it started out as superstition, he's turned it into a profitable weapon. It's a cause-and-effect matter by now. Any batter who comes up there eager to get at Hrabosky may just have to cool his heels while Al communicates with himself. The umpires have complained to him about it, but he keeps them pretty much at bay, like the hitters.

"I *am* aware I didn't mention Gibson among the great pitchers. You must know how much I think of him. Of course I'd give him highest honors. But I played alongside of him. I can't judge him the way I judge the others. Besides, he doesn't need me to confirm his ability. Ask the Yankees. Or the Red Sox. Or the Tigers. Ask the whole National League. Don't bother asking him. He doesn't have to prove anything to anybody, he was in a class by himself.

"As for the others, well, what can I say about Koufax either —more than what's already been said by how many others? Or Drysdale? They were not just fast, but fast with control, and when all is said and done, that combination is the golden one. It distinguishes the great pitchers from everybody else nearly all the time.

"I prefer to think positive thoughts about those two guys, even now that they're retired. I mean I like to remember the few happy moments they gave me rather than all the times they twisted me into a pretzel.

"One time when I was still with the Cubs, it must have been '63, I was hitting against Drysdale, who wound up and threw me the prettiest chest-high fastball you ever saw. Right down the pipe. And I missed it. *Je-sus!* I thought to myself, and then and there he gives me the same pitch on the second throw— letter-high and bright as a full moon. I whiffed at it again. Well, I stepped out of the box and said right out loud to no one in particular, 'How could I ever have missed those two pitches?'

"And John Roseboro, who was catching, said to me—disdain in his voice—'Get back in there, rook. Next one's gonna be right in the same spot.' Well, it was. And I hit it into the center-field bleachers. That's how I like to remember Drysdale. No other way, thanks.

"Oh, Maloney! *He* was your poison-dart gun! You had very little time to study anything Jumpin' Jim ever threw at you. So naturally you made a point of being maximally prepared. After going through all sorts of grief with him, one day I decided I was going to take a wood chisel to my bat and work on it so I could get the best possible grip on it. I labored on the handle of that thing for an hour and a half until there was no way it would slip out of my hands. On my first time up he came in with a pitch like a comet that broke the bat into three pieces. I coulda cried.

"Of course it's not always speed that makes an effective pitcher. Sometimes it's the ability to scare a man to death, the way Gibson used to. He'd just glare at you like he was gonna stun you with the ball, then chop your head off and cook you over an open fire.

"Or Lew Burdette. Best spitball I ever saw. Absolutely gorgeous and glistening, the real article. Or Warren Spahn, who was an unbelievable control pitcher. For twenty years running too.

"That's really the great thing about Fergie Jenkins too. He knows how to throw to a spot. That means if he knows your weakness, and most of us have one—I mean a particular place in or near the strike zone where you either can't hit with strength or accuracy, or where you're liable to swing when you shouldn't —he'll locate it with exceptional ease.

"On the other hand, the fact that Fergie throws more than occasional gopher balls is attributable to that very ability of his. Because every now and then you'll swing right at that 'wrong spot,' and then Fergie can kiss his well-placed pitch goodbye.

"Did I ever tell you about my great moment against him? Let me preface it by saying that during the 1967–68 winter we traveled around the country a lot together on business and got to be good friends.

"On opening day of 1968 we were in Chicago and Fergie was starting for the Cubs. In those days I don't think I would have done very well running for mayor of Chicago. The fans there rode me as if I was the bad guy in a movie. I guess it must have been memories of the pre-Broglio days. This one time they had a huge opening-day crowd: Every seat in Wrigley Field was taken. I was the first man up in the game of course.

"The Cub fans gave me an enormous raspberry, all 35,000 of them, and I recall thinking, 'Well, at least Fergie Jenkins likes me. He may be the only friend I have within my field of vision.' Whereupon he threw a pitch that damn near undressed me. My bat went one way and I went the other. I got up and dusted myself off, and now the crowd was cheering. Fergie's next pitch was one of those spot pitches, but I found the same spot he did, and I hit the ball out of the park. I never did ask him afterward whether he still liked me. I didn't have to ask those fans.

"Toughest to steal on? I'm not sure I care to say. Some of my secrets wouldn't be secrets if I thought there was no point in keeping them that way. But there are some guys who I derive a lot of profit from testing myself against. Let's leave it at that. Andy Messersmith, for instance, has a very quick release to first base. So has Jim Barr. And Ruthven. Sometimes that capability in a pitcher can be a pain. Like when they pick you off first base. But as I've told you over and over, when you're up against a good man, you become a good man yourself. There's no response with no challenge. When you get in a skill-on-skill contest, you stand your best chance of winning whatever it is you're trying to win—or of losing the same thing, for that matter. It's that double identity that makes the whole game so interesting. But you get what you're after only when you're up against somebody good. It does little for you to tangle with somebody you're sure you can beat. You usually end up looking about as bad as he does.

"I don't know why this puts me in mind of Dick Allen, but it does. Yeah, I guess I know why. Allen is a player who is as good as he has to be, which may sound like the standard criticism of him, but I don't mean it to be. I mean it as a compliment, because most of the time he is required to be very good and that is exactly what he is. So I'm in his corner. He is a superathlete, and a very valuable one. The proof of that is in all the efforts teams have made to get him to play for them. They wouldn't have gone after him if they didn't feel he could contribute something important to them.

"I can tell you, the biggest problem Dick Allen has had in this industry is with the media. It's not with the players. He is a hell of a lot better team man than the press gives him credit for. The question, I realize, is what is meant by 'team man.' But if you look at all that heavy-hitting talent like Luzinski and Schmidt in the Philadelphia lineup, you'll see those sluggers talking eagerly to Dick, getting pointers from him, and above all giving him their respect. When he was with St. Louis, I never saw him loaf in a game.

"Trouble is, I think, that some writer one day said to himself, 'Hey, how come Dick Allen doesn't take infield practice with the other guys? After all, a team man is a guy who comes out to the park four hours before gametime. That's my definition of it, 'cause that's the only way I ever saw the game played and that's the way it ought to be played. Therefore Allen is no team man.'

"Who's to say that's so? I played alongside Dick, and I say it ain't so. You don't see other people bound by that kind of a rule. A famous singer or actor isn't expected to put in some prescribed rehearsal schedule if he does what he does well by his own standards. Why does a professional activity like baseball have to be judged by Little League standards? I guess it must be that most of the writers have grown up with the idea that a team of players is a little like a Marine battalion, where everybody has to march in step. The press apparently wants to see to it that everybody else abides by their notion.

"Moreover, if all that practice did all that much good, how come the guys who take batting practice so religiously don't hit .400? With Dick, success is a result of raw talent, so much of it that I guess it's best to let him be the judge of how it ought to be used.

"Guys hustle on their own or they don't at all. Take Rose. You think Sparky Anderson tells Pete Rose, 'Hey Pete, I think I know how you can improve the caliber of your play. Hustle a little.'

"Pete doesn't really need that kind of counsel. He'll compete at any level, for any stakes. I recall when he and I were younger and Curt Flood was still playing, several of us had ourselves a kind of mini-conference of our own. The Leadoff Man League, sort of. We were singles hitters, mostly, so we competed among ourselves to see which of us could be the first in any season to get 200 hits or finally to earn $100,000 yearly salary. Flood got the money first, if I'm not mistaken; meanwhile I was almost disqualified in 1967, the year I hit 21 home runs.

"Well, the writers figured in this one too. Last year—'75—Pete and I were each working on our 2,500th hit. I got mine first, but I don't seem to remember that the St. Louis writers worked up much of a sweat over the fact. 'Brock steals bases.' End of story. Pete got his own number 2,500 just a little later that summer, and when he was next in St. Louis, all the writers gathered around him for an interview. And he said, 'Hey, we gotta get Lou in on this too. Between him and me we got 5,000 hits.' He thought it was a great story. I told him, 'Forget it, Pete. The writers don't agree with you.'

"Well, he didn't forget it. He won't. Neither will I. As soon as I get the 3,000th, it may help to cleanse my mind, but in the meantime I can't help nursing some doubts about the collective wisdom of the writers' fraternity.

"Of course it would be foolish to generalize about them, any more than I can generalize about, well, pitchers. There are some media people who have pride in their profession and don't let their emotions get in the way of their judgment. But everybody labors under occupational hazards, and one that sportswriters suffer from is the terrible need to pick up on something that can be turned into news, or better still, into a sensational issue. Some days there is no news and no issues. That's the way life is. Then what's a poor writer to do, especially if his editor is hungry to sell newspapers?

"*Make* the issue, is what, even if it's out of whole cloth. Just consider two items that the media are generating a lot of noise about this year, 1976.

"One of them is violence in sports. I'm not talking about hockey or football or high school basketball now. Those aren't my games. But I know something about baseball, and all the talk about the beanball war and the easy brawling in my estimation is just plain overdone. There's no more violence on the ballfield now than there ever was.

"More frankness, maybe. When the Cards were playing the Mets in April of this year and Lynn McGlothen hit Del Unser, his big mistake was admitting why he did it—to drive Unser back away from the plate. Jon Matlack admitted later he threw at Lynn himself, only Matlack's control wasn't as good as Lynn's, and he didn't hit him!

"Have you ever noticed how ballplayers, when they're interviewed or quoted in the papers, talk in generalities and cliches and don't say anything that adds up to much? They sound like dummies then, don't they? They're not. They just get very gun-shy. They know how a writer will seize on something and inflate it out of proportion, so they figure it's simply smarter policy to say something that sounds like something, only it's really nothing. That way nobody gets hurt, least of all themselves.

"Anyhow, that whole scene between the Mets and the Cardinals got blown sky-high principally because a New York team was involved and New York is where the big press is located. The writers were looking for a story, and writers, I have noticed, often operate by a sort of infection principle. In other words, if something is happening in one place or one profession or one sport, they figure it must have spread to all of them. That sounds intelligent and very heavy. Whether it's true is another matter that tends to get lost in the hysteria. Speaking of things being forgotten, don't they remember the fights the old Gas House Gang used to enjoy—and I mean enjoy! Every day too, not just now and then.

"One more thing: salaries.

"The impression is widespread today—and the writers are cultivating it—that ballplayers are overpaid. At least that some big-name players are overpaid. They're greedy, the papers are saying, they've lost the sense of the sport of the game. The old-timers didn't hang back and refuse to play if they didn't get the national treasury in return for their services; they were in baseball for the love of the game.

"What kind of hypocrisy is that? Or what kind of double standard? Does anybody on the papers offer comparable criticism of the insurance tycoon who makes a million bucks a year? Or the automobile-manufacturing executives? Or the man who discovers oil on his property and makes a fortune out of it? We say *these* guys somehow made their money by perfectly respectable methods, and maybe they did. We sure make heroes of them. We say they show initiative and drive. And we also say—I mean the people from the media say—that they are the best of their chosen fields, so they deserve what they earn.

"How many people put on a baseball uniform in America every year? Millions? Tens of thousands, anyhow, ranging from Little League kids to sandlot players and rank amateurs, up to the professionals in organized baseball. And of those, how many are pushing for those so-called impossible salaries? A couple of dozen?—the best men in their field at that, which is a damned exacting field that demands talent, experience, knowledge and hard work. Your body is just about the extent of the equipment you bring to this game, and it doesn't last you very long. You don't get the mileage out of it that corporation executives get out of their stock portfolios.

"It's a short life. And a good one. I wouldn't play ball if I didn't love it, and like most other athletes, I'll quit when it's no longer fun. But I don't feel guilty being paid for something I enjoy doing, so long as I do it well. I've seen lots of guys on the rocks just a few years after everybody was carrying them around on their shoulders. Funny how quick the shoulders turn away from them. It's not that people are fickle and cruel. It's just that somebody or something else diverts their attention. So meanwhile, you gotta make sure to keep paying attention to yourself."

11. How to steal... and 118

Lou Brock, the math major, constructed a little graph in his head, which showed one line going upward and another downward, the two intersecting. "Age and speed," he said to himself. "Savvy and reflexes. Head and legs."

Where do the lines meet, Lou?

"Not where, but when. Maybe now. Maybe any later than this is too late."

If that was an imaginary conversation at the beginning of the 1974 season, it was real by the middle of it. Come to think of it, it probably transpired years before, at least, as I said, inside Lou's head.

Writers always used to ask Brock, even back in the late

sixties, "Do you think you can break Wills' mark?" Lou would invariably say no, he didn't think so, and then he would come up with all kinds of pious reasons: Wills took a longer lead and had a matchless hook of a slide . . . nobody knew more about the art than Maury, not even Cobb; anyhow, Lou had a tendency to get a lot of extra-base hits, which diminished the number of stealing chances he had. By 1974 he could add: "Maury set his record when he was thirty. I'm now thirty-four. I'm just not as fast as I used to be. The best I've ever done was 74 stolen bases, and that's thirty less than Maury did in 1962. I'm inclined to think his mark is one of those all-time unbeatable records, like the 56 straight games DiMaggio hit safely in."

It was a litany of modesty, and as such, attractive enough to read. Yet however much a realist Brock was, and however much he was willing (more litany) to put the welfare of his team ahead of his own personal glory, no one could really believe he didn't covet what Maury Wills had done. By the end of 1973 Brock had a higher lifetime total of stolen bases than Wills had compiled in a career already finished. Besides, when you look closely at Lou, you sense a contradiction or two between what he said much of the time and the way he played all of the time. Cordial, unassuming, easygoing, all the sports stories said of him. "Third man in a two-man act," he had said of himself. "Don't try to be what you aren't."

On the other hand, and especially with his World Series performances in mind, can you think of a more intensely competitive baseball player, or one who was more dependent —not just for excellence of achievement but even for survival— on competition? In fact in his own public pronouncements, he had dwelled as often on the importance of preparation meeting opportunity, on the challenge of the moment and similar great and soaring thoughts, as he ever had on the simpler virtues of modesty and self-sacrifice.

He was *plenty* ready to make a pass at Wills' mark. Just let the opportunity appear, the challenge rise up. . . .

I'll admit this much: At the very beginning of 1974, he wasn't thinking consciously about Maury Wills or the call of destiny.

pril is a time of little flowers rather than grand designs. But just a
w days after the season began, Henry Aaron hit his 715th career
ome run, placing his name higher in the record book than that of
abe Ruth, the ultimate legend. Well, now, is there a challenge
all this or isn't there?

The graph says you're getting older and slower. It also says
u know more about life on the basepaths than you ever did.
nd you're no snail yet. The Cardinals, moreover, are pretty
uch the same ballclub this year that needed you running last
ar. You ran pretty good too, remember?

ix games passed in 1974 before Brock stole a base or, to put it
other way, before he started thinking seriously about a
gnificant increase in long-range larceny. Then suddenly, in the
an of eleven games, he stole ten times, without once getting
unned down. Almost before the rest of the league had gotten the
inks of winter ironed out of itself, Lou had copped over twenty
ases without getting caught.

He wasn't saying anything yet. The writers were doing that
r him, though as of now, in May, their talk was confined pretty
uch to wondering whether he could match the record of 42
nsecutive successful stealing attempts.

He didn't. He racked up 29 and then got nailed. This
lenced the writers momentarily, but by that time he himself was
inking bigger thoughts than they had so far taken the trouble to
xpress.

They weren't long in catching up with him. Not quite
alfway through the season—in early July, with the All-Star game
ill to be played—he had stolen his fiftieth base, for the tenth
ason in a row. Out of 56 attempts, I might add, which came to a
iccess rate of 89%, good enough for a day's pay.

The interviewers were now appearing in increasing
umbers, stage-door Johnnies bearing sweets for the sweet, and
ou began to make a point of reminding them that the Cardinals,
you please, gentlemen, were in the thick of the pennant race,
id he was just as happy about the plus-.300 batting average he

was contributing to the cause as he was of whatever number of bases he had so far heisted. (Still more litany.) Don't think he didn't know, at all times, exactly what that number was.

The johnnies were not deflected in their pursuit. "You're ahead of Wills' pace by 28 games, Lou baby."

"Uh-huh," Brock would reply, and then add: "But Maury stole 56 bases in his last 66 games."

Keep your guard up. Sleep with one eye open. Brock was a pro now who had long since learned not to take anything for granted. This was just one more respect in which he was different than the man he was now chasing: Wills—flamboyant, passionate, vain; Brock himself—cool, calculating, circumspect. Both men however, had this much in common: They were as smart as they were fast; maybe smarter. It's the smarts that make a great runner, and since we've moved Lou Brock as far as midsummer of 1974 and the All-Star break, this is probably the best time to step back for a good long look at the theoretical side of the art of base-stealing.

Article one: Get on base. First is the only base you can't steal, and although Lou has gotten there by every device in the book, respectable and otherwise—hits, walks, errors, being hit by pitches, catcher's interference, dropped third strikes—the point is, he has gotten there, plenty often. Base-stealing is no more than talk as long as you're still at the plate.

Once on first base, however, it helps to disdain it. "First base is nowhere," says Lou. "And most times it is useless to stay there. Second base is probably the safest place on the field. When I steal second, I practically eliminate the double play, and I can score on almost any hit past the infield."

So what do you do to get first base out of your system?

Let's not be in *too* much of a hurry. There's work to attend to long before you ever get on base. Remember Lou before the opening game of the 1967 World Series, when he sat quietly in the dugout and watched and thought about Jose Santiago? The picture of idleness he was, and lots of times he has been

ided by his teammates before a game—tongue in cheek, of
ourse—because of looking like a dozing malingerer. But the eyes
e always open just wide enough to pursue what he calls "my
ademics"—studying the warmup motions of the opposition's
arting pitcher. How many times has Brock hit safely on the first
tch of the game and then bolted on the second? The element of
ock is part of the strategy, to be sure—clobber your rival before
e has settled into his own rhythm—but on such occasions Lou
as often already gained some notion of that rhythm from what he
w way before the game ever began.

It *is* smooth, by God, the way he does it. And curiously slow.
t is possible to be slow *and* fast," he says. Off the ballfield Lou
ever moves quickly. He doesn't walk, he ambles. He never
rabs for things but rather extends himself in their direction. He
kes to say his favorite animal is the panther, because "it's slow
d easy all the time—a nice deceit, wouldn't you say?—except
r those moments when it's very necessary to be very fast."

That describes the stealing situation. But Lou admits—
deed he begins his disquisition on the subject with the obser-
ation—that stealing bases is theoretically improbable.

"If the pitcher-catcher combination on the one hand and the
aserunner on the other execute their respective responsibilities
erfectly, the runner will be out. It takes the runner—well, it
kes me, let's put it that way, 3.2 seconds to run from first to
cond when I get a good lead and a swift jump, when I move well
d slide at the right instant. It takes one to two tenths of a second
ss for the pitcher to set and deliver, for the catcher to catch the
all and fire it back to the second baseman with a good throw. The
nner can't win, all things being equal.

"But of course, things are never equal. Didn't somebody
nce prove that bumblebees can't fly, but never thought to tell
e bumblebees? There are a lot of ways either the runner or the
itcher can outmaneuver his rival. And the catcher and the batter
ave a say in matters too.

"Mostly, however, it's between the pitcher and me, and if
ou qualify theory with actual practice, I'm the one with most of
e advantages.

181

"In the first place, once I'm on first base, I can take a modest lead and stand perfectly still, without giving away any significant information about myself. But the pitcher is obliged to move, just to deliver the pitch, and in moving he telegraphs a whole catalog of data about himself. Furthermore, he has two things on his mind: the batter *and* me. I have only one thing in mind—to steal off him. The very business of disconcerting him is marvelously complex."

And how. I remember the day in St. Petersburg when he stole off Wilbur Wood: all the dainty little paces forward and back, the wiggles, the arm and hip movements, kicking the bag and sidling away from it and strolling back, the whole ballet. But also recalled that he never took anything approaching a long lead. And he never hit the dirt coming back to first.

"I'm left-handed, so I'm left-footed. I spring from my left foot, which gives me an advantage when I bolt to second, because I'm moving to my right. I'm at a disadvantage when I have to get back to first on a pickoff throw. So I can't afford a long lead.

"Now Maury was a rightie. He needed an extra step to get his right foot springing. But he could also get back to first faster.

"At the same time he ate a lot of dirt doing it. One of the reasons I don't like to belly-flop back to first is that most first basemen are big and strong, and when they make a tag—well, that hardly describes what they do. They don't tag you, they swing that mitt at you like a hammer. So if you're upright when you come back to first, they're likely to hit you in the midsection, where it doesn't damage you as much as if they bop you on the head, which they often do if you're down on your belly. That happened to Maury a lot. He was a beaten pulp after the '62 season.

"And not just around his top parts. He had that magnificent hook slide, which used to give second basemen and shortstops so much grief. But it made a mess of his thighs. I'd rather dive into second than dive back to first, because those guys around second are smaller, and they can't hit you the way a big first baseman can. And furthermore, a short slide isn't as rough on you as a big, sweeping hook slide.

"They used to complain about my hook, or the lack of it. When Bob Howsam was general manager of the Cardinals, he sent me a memo once saying, 'Please learn to slide!' Well, I think I learned, but I don't believe it's quite what Bob had in mind. I've found a short popup slide takes a lot less out of you."

But if you take a short lead, doesn't that mean you have farther to run, and farther still, if you go into a short popup slide instead of a long hook?

"Yeah," The laugh again. "It means I have to work harder. That's nothing new."

You mean run faster, right? But you've said you're slower now than you used to be. . . .

"No, I don't mean run faster. And while we're at it, don't make too big a deal of that diminished speed, either. I haven't lost that much. In a certain sense I never had that much. Nobody did. As I say, it isn't just a matter of how fast you can run."

It's surprise, then.

"Not likely. How much surprise do you think I can generate when I get on first base nowadays? Maybe about as much as the sun when it rises in the East. What's really surprising is if I don't make any move at all, right? Actually, the only thing the pitcher doesn't know about me is the precise moment I'm going to go, and he knows that too, damn near. You can surprise a rookie, maybe, but most of the time what you're doing is fishing in a very clear pool, where you can see the fish you're after and you lead him gently and patiently to the bait, and when he takes it, you yank.

"You just gotta know when that is, which is the part that gets to be intuitive after a while. There's no place for it in the text book. It's a little like knowing what an intimate friend is going to say a split-second before he says it. So you try to make that pitcher your very close buddy, by empathizing with all his moves and all his thoughts. You know at one point he has to commit himself, and then he can't go back on it. I have to too, but he has to first, and that makes a big difference.

"Furthermore, I can vary my moves. He can't. He depends for pitching effectiveness on a more or less regular motion. So he's an open book, while I get to keep *my* secrets—and I got more of them. So if I do my thing right—well, he and his catcher can still get me, as I said, because in a well-executed play, time is on their side. But circumstances and conditions are on mine. There's more that can go wrong between the pitcher's commitment and the second baseman's tag than can happen to me between my first spring and the moment my foot hits second base. Its percentages more than speed, and much more than surprise.

"For one thing, there's the batter. Last couple of years Ted Sizemore has been hitting behind me in the number two spot, and he and I have become a very good combination. Believe me, if you want to make base-stealing into a stock offensive weapon, as the Cardinals have decided to do, you have to set up a functioning batter-runner tandem. The hitter has to have a good eye, plus the brains and self-discipline to learn to do some things most batters wouldn't naturally do.

"He has to be willing to take a pitch, meaning to take a strike, very likely, if it's in the interests of helping the runner to make a break for second, or even to give the runner time to size up the pitcher. And he has to learn to position himself in the batter's box—the farther back the better—so that the catcher has a harder time getting off a throw. It's normal for a hitter to want to attack the ball, to move up to it, that is, away from the catcher. He has to unlearn that—in fact to move back with the pitch so that he forces the catcher to make a longer throw. He must be alert to signals, too; sometimes he can assist the runner in smelling a pitchout.

"Sizemore is excellent at all this. And he's had to be, because he's no slugger, which means they feed him fastballs more often than curves, and a fastball reduces the time you have in which to complete a steal. Furthermore, he's a right-handed hitter, and it's easier for me to take off when a leftie's hitting, because he's likely to block the catcher's view of first, and that makes it more comfortable for me to move around out there."

Lou has had some fun with that. In one game against the Philadelphia Phillies a few years back, he was on first base, with a lefthander at bat and catcher Bob Boone working behind the plate. As the pitch came in Boone suddenly heard his first baseman yell, "There he goes!" so he ripped off his mask and started to fling the ball to second. But there was nobody there, Brock was standing innocently and quite still at first base.

Brock had yelled the warning, but the catcher didn't know that, since he couldn't see first base. If he had followed through on his throw, the ball would have gone past unprotected second base into center field and Lou would have easily advanced a base. Even as it was, he got away with yelling the same thing once more before the catcher caught on, by which time he was so flustered that when Lou did break on the very next pitch—now without warning—he made it down to second with ease.

"Oh, there's lots of ways of psyching a catcher," he says. "Hell, you psych everybody. And everybody psychs you. The way of the world. I recall Jerry Grote of the Mets used to have me in the palm of his hand. He had a sixth sense about when I was going to steal. Plus he was lightning out of his crouch, and he had a fine, strong arm. He always shot me down.

"Then one day when he passed by me before a game, I decided to say hello to him. 'Hello, Grote,' I said. He didn't pay any attention to me. I said it again and he ignored me again. Then I sensed he felt better staying his distance from me, so I decided to reduce that distance whether he liked it or not. I kept saying hello to him. I could see after a while that it was eating at him, which was just fine. When I got on base I yelled 'Hello, Grote! Hello, Grote!' So he pulled off his mask and shouted back at me, 'Why don't you try it?!' I said, 'I will! I will!' And I did, on the next pitch. So whenever I see him I scream 'Grote.'

"He threw the ball into center field. He's been an easy mark ever since. You see, that was a calculated risk. If he'd beaten *me*, I'd have been *his* toy for good. But I'm free of him now."

Do you know that catchers back in the 1890s ordinarily stood in their position yards behind the batter's box? An ambitious base thief needed no Ted Sizemore in those days; he could virtually have pushed a peanut down to second with his nose and remained unmolested. They even used to score a stolen base if a runner went from first to third or from second to home on a single. Little wonder that a runner in the second half of the twentieth century needs not only legs like Brock's but a mind too—one that's just as quick, just as elastic, that covers just as much ground.

The mind, the mind . . . there's another comparison between it and the body: It is obliged to take a fearful beating too. The psychic pressure builds on any ballplayer who consciously aims at a record, and it increases mercilessly in proportion to the time required to reach that record. Some men manage this ordeal with greater ease than others, but it's an ordeal for all of them nonetheless. Henry Aaron, as naturally poised and easy-going an athlete as you might find, approached his 715th career home run with admirable cool, but he himself confessed that all the racist hate mail he got along the way sometimes made him wonder whether the effort was worth it. Maris, of course, was never really the same after 1961, when he pushed himself to the season record for round-trippers.

With the passage of the 1974 season Lou Brock himself got to know what the heat was like. As I've already mentioned, he remembered, if others forgot, that Wills sizzled during the last third of 1962, and that recollection meant that he, Brock, would not only have to keep the pressure on himself as his own year wore on, but even pump harder with every added moment of fatigue. He arrived in St. Louis one day late in the season to find a death threat waiting for him. It was a letter, too coherently, even intelligently written to be taken lightly. Worse still, it was directed at his family as well as himself. He got prompt police protection, but that stood for confinement, not just safety. Being a naturally free spirit, and independent and, as I've said, basically a private man for all his gregariousness, he hardly took kindly to the position he found himself in.

It wasn't what he had had in mind when he signed that bonus contract with the Cubs in 1960. At that time there didn't seem to be a blemish in the landscape. It may have stretched steeply uphill in front of him, but the sun shone on it so you could see all the way to the horizon, which was miles, and there were no predators hiding behind the bushes. If this, the summer of 1974, was going to be a time of glory, he would have to pay a price for it.

The death threat came to naught. At any rate, that's the way it finally read on the police blotter: case closed. But the effect in the mind of the man who is the target of that threat is not altered much by the stroke of a sergeant's pen or by the fact that the sicknik who sent the note in the first place never materialized.

Even without that episode the normal wear and tear of the baseball season was enough to take its toll. You see, there is one aspect of the record Brock was seeking which differentiates it from most other impressive individual accomplishments in baseball. It may not be a real difference, but it looks like one.

When Hornsby batted .424, when Koufax pitched his fourth no-hitter, when Ty Cobb collected more than 4,000 hits, the achievers were in all cases clearly acting in the line of duty; their records grew out of the fulfillment of their daily responsibilities.

A stolen base is not quite the same thing. It is—or rather, it appears to be—an option, not an obligation: something you may but do not have to do. If Hornsby or Cobb got three hits after his team had already taken a 10–0 lead, who could blame them? It was their job. Same with Koufax. If the Dodgers were ahead by a dozen runs, nobody expected Sandy to relent in his efforts to keep the other guy from reaching as far as first base.

But a man who tries to steal every time he gets on base may just look like what Lolich once called Lou Brock—a glory-grabber. The fact that there are all sorts of strategic justifications for stealing bases at nearly any time in a game is less obvious to the average fan. Maybe there is something intrinsically hot-dogging about stealing a base. Maybe on the other hand that notion is little more than a residue of the many years that stretched between Cobb and Wills, when baserunning was a forgotten or neglected art.

Whatever it is, Brock found himself, late in 1974, at the mercy of two pressures that pushed at him from opposite sides: one, to surpass Wills' record; the other, to avoid looking like an egomaniac in the process. There's no way you can strike a compromise between those two forces, since they are in conflict. So Lou did pretty much what you'd expect him or any other reasonable man to do. He went for the record. Not to go for it would be the height of idiocy. And he kept his cool, husbanded his energies, took care of himself, didn't brood, made sure to keep out of the way of the swinging mitts of big first basemen, likewise to maintain his leg-saving popup slide. Likewise, for that matter, to keep his eye clear. For he needed the hits. He could be sure no one was going to put him on first base by charity.

July turned into August, and Brock's stolen-base total grew steadily, under the pressure he himself was adding from within to all the others that came from without. Seventy bases . . . 80 . . . 90 . . . 94 . . . ten to go to tie the record, eleven to break it. . . . September . . . 100, 101 . . .

Maury Wills watched all this from Los Angeles, and the way he responded to it warms my heart. He was not happy, and he didn't mind saying so. As it became more and more likely Brock would replace him in the record book—there was still a month of playing time left in the season—he took an attitude which to me is as rational as Brock's: He grieved over the winnowing away of the single accomplishment in which he had taken the greatest pride. There was no resorting to sentimentalized cliche ("Records are made to be broken, fellas, and I've enjoyed my little moment front and center, so let somebody else have it now"). Wills was not only smart but honest. "You don't think Hemingway or Michelangelo would have been delighted to see their achievements surpassed, do you?" he said. And then he added that he didn't wish Brock ill, in fact he admired him. It was just that he didn't like to give up what was precious and hard-earned, and so far as I'm concerned, that's a perfectly healthy outlook. Lou, just as smart, just as honest, thought so too.

On September 10, Brock's stolen-base total stood at 103. One shy. There was a single night game left in the Cardinals' homestand, following which they would be on the road for two weeks. The leaves were starting to turn along the Mississippi, and the withering St. Louis heat didn't wither quite so much as it had a month earlier. The season was getting on. Now was The Time.

Lou wanted to break the record in front of the hometown folks, who felt exactly the same way about it. "Nobody was in the dark about anything," he said. "It was a perfect situation."

Dick Ruthven found it eminently clear. He was the starting pitcher for the Phillies that night, and already well into a successful season. As solicitous as anyone of securing a place for his name in the record book, he was not, however, eager to see it there because he had been the pitcher of record when Lou Brock broke the major league stolen-base record. He happened to have a pitching motion that Lou had always found troublesome. And he meant to put it to optimal use tonight.

Brock figured he had no more choice in the matter than Ruthven. And, being the kind of man he is, he acted on that recognition with all deliberate haste. He drove a single to left field to open the home first. He watched Ron Hunt (Sizemore was out with a bad ankle) take a strike.

Then he let her rip. Bob Boone, the Philly catcher, reacted quickly, but in effect, too quickly, his throw plunking Lou and going into center field, and Brock—well, he went into an epochal tie with Maury Wills.

Ruthven hung in. In fact he pitched well enough to keep Brock and all the Cardinals subdued well into the game. In the seventh inning, however, Lou cracked another hit into the same left-field spot. Ron Hunt repeated his own earlier motions by swinging at and missing Ruthven's first pitch.

Now.

Brock edged away to his favored three-and-a-half-step lead while Ruthven peered at him. The old cat-and-mouse dance: a throw to first; runner back safely; leads again; is coaxed back again; leads . . . and flies.

Boone's throw this time was right where it should have been, except that Brock's foot was too, and it got there first.

Busch Stadium erupted. Thirty thousand voices chanted *Lou! Lou! Lou!* The whole Cardinal team poured out of the dugout and the bullpen and onto the field. Play was halted while somebody dislodged the second-base bag and handed it to Lou. Somebody else dragged a microphone out to the infield. Cool

Papa Bell appeared, one of the fastest men who ever played in the old Negro leagues. (You've come a long way, baby.) He made a little congratulatory speech. And Brock made a little speech of his own. And the crowd cooed *Lou*, *Lou*, *Lou* again and people posed for photographs. And St. Louis was the center of the universe.

Don't run off. I have something to add, which is not so much of an afterthought as it sounds. Brock tried one more theft that night, in the ninth inning, with the Cardinals behind, 6–2. Boone threw him out. After the game, which the Phils won by that margin, the young catcher remarked to the press that he had lost some respect for Brock when Lou made that last try.

Brock reacted. The cool was gone, washed away in a flood of relief and depressurization, but the mind—and now the tongue—were razor-sharp.

"Did I ever say I cared whether he had respect for me? Who is to say, dammit, when you can steal a base and when you can't? I very much doubt that Bob Boone made the rule.

"Look. We were down by six. Ruthven had us where the hair is short. Wouldn't you want to break his grip any way you can? Isn't a stolen base the best thing I can come up with to break a pitcher's rhythm? Haven't we been over all this before? Hell, you do it whenever you can, whether you're in a 1–1 game in the fifteenth inning or behind by a thousand runs in the third."

Later Lou added: "Aw, Boone was young. He had his values mixed up, that's all. Besides, what he was watching there, let me be frank, was an event, and not just a game. Mike Schmidt later said, 'Well, Lou broke the record, but we still kicked their butts.' That makes better sense than what Boone said, 'cause Schmidt was caught up in the competitive spirit of the moment. But you know, if you had asked anyone a year later, what the final score of the game Lou Brock broke the base-stealing record in, do you think they'd remember it? They'd remember *105*; I doubt anyone could recall the score."

12. MVP Disappointment... On to Cobb and 3000 Hits

Anyone reading this far would have to allow that fate has been good to Lou Brock, plenty good. There aren't too many sharecropper's sons who hit .391 in Series play. Or who, for that matter—before 1974 was done—had stolen thirteen bases in addition to the 105 we just finished discussing. (Somewhere along here the number 118 has to be repeated, for documentation's sake.) Brock has made it by skill, all right, and by hard work, but he's had more than his share of luck too, overall.

Underline "overall," to allow for an exception here and there. You can't regard Lou as an ingrate or a pouter if he remains just as mindful of the occasions when fortune deserted him as of those when she took him in her loving arms.

She's given him some chilly moments. Why did he fail to win the Most Valuable Player award in 1974? Or do you think luck had nothing to do with that? They'll argue the issue for years to come, no doubt, and the folks from L.A. who justifiably admire Steve Garvey will justifiably cite the myriad contributions he made to the Dodger pennant that year. He was more than fortunate, they'll say. He deserved the award and he got it.

Still, how would you feel if you came from St. Louis? Or if you were Lou Brock himself, with a year immediately behind you that happens to one player in ten thousand?

You mention, sympathetically, that he broke Wills' record right at the time the nation was most deeply engrossed in the catastrophe of Watergate and all it implied. Richard Nixon had resigned the presidency in August. By September 10 the shock of that event still reverberated with such force that every other news item, it seemed, got swept into the back pages of the papers. Would Brock's achievement have been page-one stuff in more halcyon days?

"Maybe," he says. "Maybe not. If all the noise about Watergate drew attention away from me, it had the same effect on other ballplayers. Besides, I suspect I wouldn't have made the front page during any other time either.

"What worked against me in the MVP balloting was not a simple matter, but I can't help thinking a good deal of it had to do with the old prejudice we've discussed before about base-stealers . . . you know, that they do it for personal gain, not for the welfare of the team, so how can you call them 'valuable'? I think it's nonsense, but what's done is done."

Then he grinned. "There's discrimination against us thieves. We really ought to start a campaign to upgrade our image. 'Larceny Lib,' we could call it. Or 'Banditry is Beautiful.' "

You're laughing about it now, Lou. You weren't at the end of the 1974 season or early 1975, when you lost the award.

"You're right about the laughing. You're wrong about losing it. It's true I didn't win it, but it's not true I lost it. I earned it. Of that I am convinced, and it's enough for me. What really ticked me off was when several of those writers called me up right after the voting to say how sorry they were to hear I hadn't got the award. The fact was, they had placed me no higher on their own ballots than sixth or seventh. I found that out later. I call it bush."

Lou enunciated those words with a staccato emphasis that seemed foreign to all I had read and much I had learned about him. Friendly lighthearted Lou, Mr. Velvet, had in fact some pretty sharp, indeed jagged, metallic edges inside himself that sometimes cut his own vitals. I used a different simile some pages back, scar tissue, to convey the same idea. It bears repeating here. Yes, he has been a fortunate man, and he has climbed high. But along the way he has picked up his share of bruises and lacerations. This day he was rubbing them tenderly.

It was a day early in 1975 when 1974 was still very much with him. He hadn't fully come down from it yet. It had been the critical passage of his adult life: the season with the highest ups and the lowest downs and the most money riding on it. A magnificent time it was, a prodigy of a year, but it had smacked him around and bounced him off the wall about as much as it had swept him up into reaches where he lost his breath from excitement.

He would never use words like this to describe it. I don't think he would even conceive of it this way. The self-control and internal discipline which have enabled him to transform a bunch of curiously mixed talents and weaknesses into one of the most concentrated packages of all-round competence and competitiveness in modern professional athletics would never permit him to linger upon himself this way. It is one thing to subject one's gifts and drawbacks alike to analysis, then to compose them, and turn the result into energy; it's another to subject one's very capacity for analysis to more analysis. That's like holding a mirror up to a mirror. There's no profit in it. You can leave it to the writers. The only trouble with that, of course, is that you are at the mercy of what they may say, and they can make mistakes about you. Didn't he know it!

Meanwhile, don't forget that during 1974 his marriage to

Katie Brock had finally come clattering apart. The divorce was inevitable, and the split from the kids: Wanda , now at the vulnerable edge of adolescence, and Lou Jr., still a wide-eyed pup. He loves them. Again, he would not dwell on it beyond the tersest acknowledgment of the fact, but the adjustment to singleness after more than a decade of family life—and a dim memory or two of the broken home he himself had coped with in his early years—took some doing.

Well, what does it all come down to then but another and different kind of challenge? So do as you have always done. Accept it.

First of all, come down, gently down, from the '74 high. Take some time to enjoy the off-season. Arrange it so you see Wanda and little Lou as often as possible. Pleasure yourself in them, give of yourself and don't grieve over their lot and yours, for that's the worst thing you can do for all three of you.

Have a little fun on the banquet circuit. You have a lot of stories to tell, and it's no pain to see that ocean of faces out there, each of them fixed upon you and keenly following all the memories which you are, to begin with, uniquely equipped to recount in the most meticulous detail. Tell them about 1974, and while you're at it, tell them about the Broglio deal too, and the Polo Grounds home run, and the '67 Series and the one in '68, and the fourteen bases you stole in both of them. Take the art of the steal apart, like a good surgeon lecturing on anatomy. Help the faces understand this least understood of baseball stratagems, this special baseball thrill. Tell them what it's like to be Lou Brock. They care.

Make some business deals. You got a hell of an agent, Jack Childers, up in Chicago, who you've known for a long time. Do some commercials. Design a shoe for the Converse people, say, with a special sole that enhances the lateral traction a base-thief needs when he makes his break for second. Call it the Lou Brock 118 model. Why not? And what the hell . . . get an art critic to write a book about you. While you're busy with all this, don't forget to enjoy the fact that *The Sporting News* called you the top male athlete of 1974. That's worth a warm inner glow or two.

t's time for St. Pete and spring training, and this is just about
where we came in, March of 1975. The season that followed for
Lou Brock was marred by injuries, not the least of which was the
damage he did to his shoulder as a result of that unbelievable
catch of the Bill Madlock line drive which I narrated in the opening pages. Still, Lou hit his expected .309, and stole his quota
of fifty-plus bases for the eleventh year in a row.

And summer became fall, which became winter, then
spring. It was the 100th anniversary of the National League.
Fitting for some new challenge, wouldn't you say, some
unprecedented meetings of preparation and opportunity.

One of them was obvious, of course; tough, but obvious.
Tyrus Raymond Cobb, the Georgia Peach, who owned several of
the most awesome records in the book and who may have been
the best player in the history of the galaxy, stole 892 bases in his
lifetime. At the outset of 1976, Lou Brock had 809, the most ever
for a National Leaguer, more than Honus Wagner or Eddie
Collins or Max Carey or anybody. Anybody but Cobb.

Can you do it, Lou? Better still, can you do it in one season?
You're thirty-six going on thirty-seven, baby; it would take all of
84, and that's a carload.

"You don't seem to understand, even after all this time," he
said, a smile dancing on his lips. "It would be nice. Oh, it would
be *fine*. But have you forgotten I'm a hitter too? Why don't you
ask me about getting my 3,000th career hit?"

O.K., how about your 3,000th hit? Seems to me there are
eleven other guys who got there before you.

"But how many of them got that many hits, *plus* 800-some
stolen bases? Frankly, I don't want to go down in history as just a
sprinter. I own a bat too, and I think it's time people got around to
realizing that I know how to use it. My goal, my priority is still to
reach 3000 hits. But between now and 3000, there are going to be
a lot of cries of: 'There he goes!' "

Just a sprinter, mind you. And now he wants 3,000 hits, as if
that's the ice cream and 893 bases is the maraschino cherry. This
guy really does like a challenge.

"Yeah. You bet." The smile vanished. "I also like my options.

Where do you think I'd be if I had decided to let it all ride on just one thing I could do? I love variety. You know that."

And the unpredictable. Well, Lou might just do it. Whether he does or not, it'll be a smashing contest to watch: fate and old devil time pitted against the most elegant pro alive, who always knew a gauntlet when he saw one, but who, having seen it thrown before him, never failed to pick it up.

It's just that he wants to do it his way. Elusive, and his own man, to the end. Last time I saw him, he was driving me from his place to the St. Louis airport in his elegant, unbelievable Stutz Blackhawk, a custom-made mansion of a motor car with 24-karat gold dashboard equipment. We pulled into a gas station for some fuel. The goggle-eyed attendant sized up the Stutz, recognized Lou and quietly flipped.

"That is some mother," he said. "I don't mean to be personal, but, uh, how much that baby run you?"

"About 120 miles an hour," said Lou.

13.
Afterword.
A Brock
Fan Club: Musial.
Schoendienst.
and Banks.

STAN MUSIAL

"The year I was general-manager of the Cardinals, 1967, we won the pennant and the World Series, but please give me credit for helping win in '64 too.

"I didn't play that year. If I had, I'm not at all sure we could have gone all the way. But by retiring at the end of '63 I put pressure on the St. Louis management to find somebody new for their outfield. They came up with Lou Brock, and he's what made the difference between first place and everything else. Wouldn't you agree the Cardinals owe me a small debt of gratitude for getting out of the way?

"They owe Lou a bigger one. For my money he has been the most exciting baseball player in the major leagues over the last ten years. I can't count the times I've seen him transform a whole stadium full of people just by walking to the plate. You never know what he's going to do, except it's likely to be both interesting and good. It might be an opposite-field blooper that drops in or a towering home run. Furthermore, it's not just that any single he hits is potentially a double; it's that getting that second base by stealing it is charged with so much more excitement than just blasting a long line drive off the wall. But he may blast one that way too. That's why I think his base-stealing accomplishments are so extraordinary. He hits for extra bases so often that it actually cuts down on his opportunities for stealing.

"I don't think Lou or anybody else believed Maury Wills' mark would topple after only twelve years. It looked like one of those 'eternal' records. After all, what Maury did was magnificent. And there's no doubt Lou had to have everything going for him in '74 to do even better. He had to hit consistently; he had to have a good team in back of him and a savvy guy like Ted Sizemore hitting right behind him. He had to have a lot of plain good luck. And he got it. All those ingredients worked with remarkable coordination.

"But don't forget he had to have skill too, and understanding. And I suppose everyone agrees that what finally mattered most of all was that understanding of his, that exceptional knowledge of the game in general and baserunning in particular that he had worked so hard to achieve over the years.

"Baseball today is not the same game I broke into in the early forties, and Lou's career is a kind of brilliant testimony to the change. Over the past couple of decades most of the old ballparks have come down; they've been replaced by big, shiny plants with larger playing areas and more distant fences. So it's been hard on the sluggers. But it's created a new kind of fast action in which baserunning counts for more than it did in the old days. That means a new species of ballplayer, a swift, versatile, resourceful type who can hit and run and above all think while he's at it.

"Lou Brock typifies that player. Even more, he is the model of it, one of the very best of the breed. When they finally do the

history of this era, his name is going to be written in large letters.
He's a friend of mine, and I'm proud to know him. But in a larger
sense, he's one of baseball's prizes. The game has been good to
him, but he's more than repaid its favors."

RED SCHOENDIENST

"I got the sense of him that day in Houston in '64, when he first
showed up in a St. Louis uniform. Bing Devine traded with the
Cubs for him just before the June 15 deadline, and Brock was with
us by the end of the next day. Gangling kid with his glove in his
hand, jogging toward the dugout, just in from Chicago. I can still
see him. Anybody who wanted to be with the Cardinals that badly
had to have something going for him, I figured.

"I knew he was a good player, even when he was with the
Cubs. A rookie trying to hold down right field in Cubs Park was
bound to have a hard time of it. The sun is bad in your eyes
out there, and the wind runs in circles in the outfield. I guessed it
was just a matter of time before he got the hang of it. Fortunately
for us, that happened in St. Louis. I don't think you can fault the
Cubs too much for that Broglio deal. They needed pitching and it
looked as though they were going to get it. We needed an
outfielder and it looked as though *we* were going to get it. Turned
out only one of us was right.

"Yeah, Lou likes to be alone, but don't make too much of
that. He's a happy guy, as I see it. At least he is in the clubhouse,
where I'm in touch with him. He's cool and easy, even if things
might not be going his way.

"Of course mostly they go his way, or at least he sees to it
they do. He'll break all those records he's after, I've no doubt of it.
He's that kind of guy, that durable a player, that good a body. He
has his faults, sure. It's true about him in the outfield. He
sometimes has a hard time with ground balls hit to his right.
Dunno why; maybe he opens his glove when he ought to be
closing it. But I'd like more players with his kind of problems, if
they had just half his gifts.

"He doesn't strike out nearly as much as he used to, by the

way. He's a learner. In fact, sometimes you have to keep him on a leash, he's so eager to better himself. I really think he ought to leave that new switch-hitting ambition of his alone. If he wanted to bat both ways he should have perfected it long ago. He's better off against lefties just hitting left-handed, as he always has. He's serious about his motives too, I'm sure. In fact, the reason he's not a switch-hitter today is because the Cubs discouraged him early in his career. God knows he's always trying to improve himself.

"But he'll make it just being the old Brock. I remember '74. He did that one all by himself, with no outside help. I never had a sign for him to steal. I had one that told him not to, but I don't think I used it more than a couple times all season.

"I can't think of anything else to say about him. He just loves to play ball. If you could as well as him, wouldn't you?"

ERNIE BANKS

"Ah, to be thirty-seven again! Why, he's just gettin' started. Sure he's gonna break Cobb's record. He takes such good care of himself and he's so smart—why, I just don't see how he can miss.

"Unless . . . well, you know, there *is* another side of Lou Brock that I remember from the old Cub days, and I don't think he's changed all that much in the meantime. What I mean is he is underneath all the good times a powerfully serious young man, and a serious disposition means you can be a victim of stress. Stress can be a mean mother. If Lou feels too much of it—and I've seen it eat at him now and then—he could have a pretty hard time with that record.

"I ain't worried about him, 'cause he can take care of himself. But that doesn't change the fact that he's a complex guy. You see, he's a Gemini. The Twins are working, always working with Lou, and sometimes one of them fights the other: Mr. Outside collides with Mr. Inside. He feels a lot more than he ever says. I know. I watched him plenty when he came up to Chicago, partly because he was my roomie, and partly because he was such a bundle of talent you naturally couldn't keep your eyes off him.

"Well, he was plenty uptight when he arrived. I recall him sayin': 'Ernie, I just *gotta* make it! I can't afford *not* to make it!' That's when I saw that fantastic motivation already cookin' in him. No single thing about him is more responsible for his success.

"On the other hand, you see—here's the other Twin—that tension took its toll too. I used to tell him, the harder you try, Lou, the worse you're gonna get.

"I was partly right, partly wrong. He finally did make it, didn't he? And his way, by never lettin' up, always pushin' to make himself better. You sure can't argue with the results, can you?

"At the same time, he did finally learn to relax. I remember the moment it happened, at least the moment I saw it take hold. It was right after that big blast of a home run in the Polo Grounds in 1964.

"Why, you wouldn't have recognized him, I swear. Lou Brock, mind you, sober, hard-workin', out-to-the-ballpark-at-eight-in-the mornin' Lou Brock, our own best boy scout. It was like somebody had let him out of a cage. He flew around that dugout like a bird, chirpin' away, gigglin', slappin' people on the back, tiltin' his head back and lettin' his arms hang loose, and *laughin'*, man, havin' himself a real live ball, first one I ever saw him have since he was with the Cubs. He was a free man. It did my heart good, and I think everybody else's. He was really a little crazy. How he needed that!

"And how he talked! Have you listened to Lou talk? He's a, well, I don't know that he's a *genius* talker exactly, but he's awful good with words. I could sit and listen to him read the phone book. And he has the thoughts to go with the words, the kind of sensitive mind that ties in with that seriousness I told you about. He knows people. He has feelers a mile long. Maybe that's why he's good at figurin' out pitchers.

"In fact, that's what I see he has in common with Maury Wills. People like to contrast Lou and Maury—what's different about them. You know: Lou has the short slide, Maury the great broad hook, etc. Well, I think they're much more alike than different, because the best thing about both of them is not their talent, or their speed, or their runnin' or slidin' style, or anything like that. It's their brains. I've seen Lou—and Maury—both psych out a pitcher as if they were inside the man's head, just readin' the meter.

"And after the smarts, it's their motivation. Both of them wanted tremendously hard to get where they are.

"Maybe Lou is faster. I guess he must be, since he always takes a shorter lead and a shorter slide. Has to be somethin' to make up for the difference, wouldn't you say? Also, sometimes I think maybe Lou has taken lessons in the martial arts. On the sly maybe. He moves like a man who knows Tae Kwan Do. Short and sudden. First all quiet, then *whomp!* Like a cat pouncin'. Actually, like a panther. That's his favorite animal, you know that? He just sits back very still, lookin' like a statue. Then all of a sudden he leaps, and you sit there, wonderin' how anyone can move from zero velocity to the speed of light like that.

"He's the same way in the outfield. Just the other night on TV, I saw Kingman hit a sinkin' liner to left. There wasn't anybody near that ball. Then, in half a flash, Lou had it in his glove. It was like there must have been some frames missin' from the TV film. *Old* Lou, hell! He's as fast at thirty-seven as he ever was.

"The Broglio deal? What Broglio deal? I don't want to talk about that. Nobody on the Cubs wants to talk about that. That deal never occurred, you understand? What is there to say about something that never happened?

"I'll tell you what I'll talk about. His value to the St. Louis Cardinals *off* the basepaths and out of the batter's box.

"Lou knows how to excite people. He *makes* response. And I swear he has a system figured out. He does it one way when the Cardinals are winnin' and another way when they're losin'.

"When things are runnin' smoothly, he'll show up in the locker room lookin' kind of 'peekid', real slow and lethargic, and distant. He looks a little sick, and people wonder, what's ailin' Lou?

"Then the game starts, and suddenly he's a whirlwind. Since he's leadoff man, he sets the pace, and he goes zippin' out there as if he was the chief of the fire department. Oftentimes he'll swing at the first pitch, and almost as often he gets on. And you know what happens when he gets on.

"It takes everybody by surprise, and aside from bein' relieved to see he's his old self, they just look at him with their mouths open, wonderin' how such a transformation could take place. But then, you see, they start to imitate him. They play like hell. He doesn't give anyone a chance to lay back and get bored.

"Contrarily, when things are goin' bad, he's alive from the time he walks into the clubhouse. He kids around, plays it light, like a kitten.

"But all this time he's a loner. *I* never forget that. Yet he's also such a studious, thinkin'-kind of guy that he quite consciously turns on the charm and dazzle when he wants to, especially when he thinks it's goin' to help the ballclub.

"Anyhow, he likes the element of surprise, so he often makes a point of behavin' exactly the opposite of the way you'd normally think he ought to behave in view of any misery the team, or himself, might be goin' through. I've seen him many times achin' all over from some injury, but a lot more than he ever lets on.

"So anyhow, durin' that losin' spell, Lou functions on the diamond the way he does in the locker room. He stirs up fun, plays all the infield spots durin' pregame warmups, just for the hell of it, hits right-handed instead of left—anythin' to get his teammates diverted.

"Yeah, he's a psychologist. He knows which of his own club members are secretly—or maybe not so secretly—envious of him. And he's sure enough of his own abilities that he's willin' to play on that envy by gettin' the guy who feels it to want to perform better, out of a sheer sense of rivalry with Lou. I've seen him nag and needle a guy 'til the guy sort of says to himself, 'O.K., Brock,

I'll show you I can run as fast as you, or hit to the opposite field as good as you can.' Lou knows that while the guy is out there tryin' to show him up, he might just be playin' better for the Cardinals in the process. And Lou's enough of a businessman to know that when the team performs well, regardless of the reason, it finally means a sweeter deal for himself. Man, I admire that kind of a head.

"I never had it. I wasn't disciplined enough to think that way, which reminds me that I learned a lot from him when we were together in Chicago. From the very start, even when he was a rookie, he had a fantastically orderly mind. He was a real student of the game. He could never have turned *me* into the walkin' encyclopedia of facts and figures that he was, but he taught me how much his own careful study of the game contributed to makin' him into a better ballplayer. I realized how much of this game can be mental. I used to like to watch him pick up the papers in the mornin', then go over all the sports stories so he could find out who was doin' what. He not only knew all the averages, but who was hurt and what part of him was hurtin'. He knew that if he played against the hurt guy he could take advantage of the injury somehow. And the older he's got, the more advantages he's learned to take.

"We had a nice time of it together, Lou and me. He was easy to live with because he, well, like I said, basically Lou's a solitary man and didn't impose himself on others. He didn't care much for the flashy nightspots where many of the players would congregate on a road trip. It was enough to go out for a quiet dinner somewhere, maybe to a spot where there was some good jazz. We liked to go to Small's in Harlem. And Lou would sip his Coca-Cola. Never drank. Clean liver.

"And I'll tell you, if he didn't like a guy he'd just stay away from him. No fights, no mean words. He'd just slip away. He may be easy for most people to like, but he has his own standards. He likes reliable people. Anybody who promises him something and doesn't deliver—even if he's late for an appointment—well, Lou will say nothin'; he'll just drift away from the guy.

"If he likes you, on the other hand, he'll work damn hard for you, without ever givin' up that precious privacy of his. And he's a good judge of people, of their sensitivities. Just as I said he could ride some of his own teammates, you know, goad them into playin' better just to spite *him*, he could also jolly them along and give them tons of moral support if he supposed that was the best way to help them. I saw him do that much for proud, established men like Gibson and Hrabosky, just as he did for rookies. I saw him work endlessly to give pointers to Ken Reitz and Ted Sizemore and Mike Tyson. He played all those guys like a good outfielder plays a fly ball off the wall.

"Let me add one more thing about his heart. He gave it to the kids. Ain't no player in the major leagues has done more for kids than Lou Brock. He started boys' clubs in St. Louis—in the black community and the white community alike. There must be a couple of generations of young guys in St. Louis who think of Lou Brock as a sort of a king.

"But he never let up with that competitive instinct of his. Do you remember how they used to boo him in Wrigley Field? I don't mean just back in the early days. Then they razzed him because he was such an ox in the outfield. They expected a lot of him, and he never lived up to what they thought he was able to do.

"Later on, though, when he fulfilled all that talent, they *really* got on his back. If he took an extra breath, they'd boo him. I think it was mostly because Lou did such a mean and consistent job of beating the socks off the Cubs. He loved to beat us, and he made an extra-special effort to do so. The Bleacher Bums in Wrigley Field knew that, so they gave *him* an extra-special kind of hell. They were just sore 'cause he wasn't playin' on their side. It's like the way they get all over Pete. Rose. It's actually a compliment to Brock and Rose—those spectators in Chicago know how good those two guys are and how hard they play.

"Yeah, I think he should have won the MVP in '74. I don't know what Lou says about that now, but I know it cut him to the quick then, and I remember him sayin' if they gave him the award the next year, he wouldn't accept it. He didn't win points among the press with that remark. But he spoke his mind. Like I said, the stress gets to him at times, no matter how easygoin' he looks.

"I guess I'm prejudiced. I like Lou a lot . . . and Steve Garvey is a fine man and a fine ballplayer, but I can't help thinkin' Steve got the MVP largely 'cause the Dodgers have such a high-powered publicity apparatus. They got the press out there in L.A. It's Media City, damn near, just like New York. Any player in either town has an automatic jump on anybody from a smaller place. St. Louis just can't rev up that kind of machinery. Sure, I've heard Lou say he doesn't buy that theory. *I* buy it. Anyhow, you know, he won the Sporting News Player of the Year award in 1974. That's some consolation, isn't it? Maybe it isn't, come to think of it. Not for a competitor like Lou. He wants to fly with the angels. Anything lower than that is, well, it just ain't the angels.

"In my book that record, that stolen-base record, is somethin' tremendous, but it ain't all that Lou Brock is. He's—he's just all ballplayer. When I see him run from the dugout out to left field, I say, 'Now that's as pretty a baseball sight—just that guy runnin' out to his position—as you'd ever want to see.' "